Foreign Direct Investment

Foreign Direct Investment

Smart Approaches to Differentiation and Engagement

DANIEL NICHOLLS

Routledge
Taylor & Francis Group

LONDON AND NEW YORK

First published in paperback 2024

First published 2012 by Gower Publishing

Published 2016 by Routledge
4 Park Square, Milton Park, Abingdon, Oxon OX14 4RN

and by Routledge
605 Third Avenue, New York, NY 10158

Routledge is an imprint of the Taylor & Francis Group, an informa business

Publisher's Note
The publisher has gone to great lengths to ensure the quality of this reprint but points out that some imperfections in the original copies may be apparent.

British Library Cataloguing in Publication Data
Nicholls, Daniel.
   Foreign direct investment : smart approaches to differentiation and engagement.
   1. Investments, Foreign. 2. Intercultural communication – Economic aspects. 3. Communication in economic development. 4. Business communication – Political aspects.
   I. Title
   658.1'52-dc23

Library of Congress Cataloging-in-Publication Data
Nicholls, Daniel.
   Foreign direct investment : smart approaches to differentiation and engagement / by Daniel Nicholls.
      p. cm.
   Includes bibliographical references and index.
   ISBN 978-1-4094-2357-7 (hardback)   ISBN 978-1-4094-2358-4 (ebook)
   1. Investments, Foreign. I. Title.

   HG4538.N494 2012
   332.67'3–dc23
                                                      2012023915
ISBN: 978-1-4094-2357-7 (hbk)
ISBN: 978-1-03-283687-4 (pbk)
ISBN: 978-1-315-58275-7 (ebk)

DOI: 10.4324/9781315582757

Contents

List of Figures and Table   *vii*

About the Author   *ix*

Acknowledgements   *xi*

List of Abbreviations   *xiii*

Introduction   1

1   FDI in a Downturn: Trends and Lessons Learned   7

2   Place Brands: 'Guarantors' of Investment   27

3   Protectionism and Neo-imperialism   43

4   The Investor Perspective   57

5   Politics and Public Diplomacy   69

6   Where Next for FDI?   79

Bibliography   97

Index   103

List of Figures and Table

FIGURES

I.1a	FDI destination market heat map – capital investment 2006–2008	2
I.1b	FDI destination market heat map – capital investment 2009–2011	2
Chapter 1 image	Dubai: a city built on more than sand	6
1.1	Global FDI flows, average 2005–2007 and 2007–2011	8
1.2	Africa's GDP growth far exceeds population growth	24
Chapter 2 image	Egypt and the Tahrir Square protests	26
2.1	Open city, open brand	30
2.2	A visual representation of Brand Switzerland, as defined by the Federal Department of Foreign Affairs	36
Chapter 3 image	Dubai Ports World	42
Chapter 4 image	Old Street Roundabout, East London	56
4.1	Drivers of R&D investments by location	60

Chapter 5 image   Joining the club   68

Chapter 6 image   Designed in Africa   78

6.1   Top lead-generation channels   81

6.2   Channels for acquiring a customer   81

6.3   The MICE approach to social media   82

TABLE

Table 6.1   The link between FDI, talent and brand   88

About the Author

Daniel is a senior consultant at the economic development consultancy OCO Global in London, where he works on a variety of consulting and training assignments for clients and industry associations. His recent client work has included the auditing and finessing of sector propositions for UK Trade & Investment, training for Enterprise Florida and strategic consulting for Invest in Fife. He has also led the development of OCO's thought leadership and insight programme, authoring and editing numerous papers and reports on FDI-related topics, from place branding and financial services to talent attraction and retention and the rise of renewable energy.

With a background in marketing and communications, Daniel has lived and worked in various European countries over the past decade, including France, Poland, Belgium and Hungary. He began his career in Brussels, where he worked for the think-tank Friends of Europe and the public affairs consultancy Policy Action before moving to Budapest to work for the PR firm Mmd (later renamed Grayling), where he worked on assignments across Central and Eastern Europe and the Middle East, including a global audit of Abu Dhabi's brand and investment reputation. On returning to the UK, Daniel joined the global PR firm Hill & Knowlton as Marketing and Business Development Manager for Europe, Middle East and Africa (EMEA). As part of his programme to raise the firm's profile in the region, he collaborated with the Common Market for Eastern and Southern Africa (COMESA) during its 2010 Investment Forum in Egypt.

He is a regular speaker at international FDI seminars and conferences such as those organised by the European Association of Development Agencies (EURADA) and Red Hot Locations. His work has also featured in the *Financial Times*'s specialist bi-monthly *fDi Magazine*.

Acknowledgements

My first thanks go to the global leadership of Hill+Knowlton Strategies who originally gave me the opportunity to write this book. Particular thanks go to Lalu Dasgupta and Andrew Laurence who both provided thoughts and guidance on various PR-related aspects of FDI during the early stages of writing. Thanks also go to my more recent employer OCO and various colleagues there, including Ian Rooks, Judith Walker and Ryan O'Lynn who provided their comments, insight and support. I am also grateful both to *fDi Magazine*'s Editor, Courtney Fingar, as well as the Executive Director of the World Association of Investment Promotion Agencies (WAIPA), Carlos Bronzatto, for reviewing various parts of my book while it was in progress.

I would also like to thank the various individuals and organisations which have kindly provided me with images and other graphics for this book, including: the United Nations Conference on Trade and Development (UNCTAD), Copenhagen Capacity, Switzerland's Federal Department of Foreign Affairs, Dubai Ports World, UK Trade & Investment, the Ministry of External Affairs of India, HubSpot, OCO, fDi Intelligence, VMK Plc. and Marwa Sameer Morgan.

Sincere thanks also go to Jonathan Norman, Fiona Martin, Emily Ruskell and the team at Gower Publishing for all of their support, guidance and ultimately their patience.

My final thanks go to my family, friends and Chris for all their support throughout the project.

List of Abbreviations

BRICS   Brazil, Russia, India, China and South Africa

CEE   Central and Eastern Europe

CELAC   Community of Latin American and Caribbean Countries

CIS   Commonwealth of Independent States

CIVETS   Columbia, Indonesia, Vietnam, Egypt, Turkey and South Africa

EAC   East African Community

ECLAC   Economic Commission for Latin America and the Caribbean

EDO   Economic Development Organisation

EIU   Economist Intelligence Unit

EMEA   Europe, Middle East and Africa

EURADA   European Association of Development Agencies

FDI   Foreign Direct Investment

FIFA   Fédération Internationale de Football Association

FMCG   Fast-moving Consumer Goods

FTA   Free Trade Agreement

GDP	Gross Domestic Product
IEDC	International Economic Development Council
IMF	International Monetary Fund
IOM	International Office for Migration
IPA	Investment Promotion Agency
IPO	Initial Public Offering
JV	Joint Venture
MENA	Middle East and North Africa
MERCOSUR	Mercado Común del Sur (Common Southern Market)
N11	Next Eleven
NAFTA	North American Free Trade Agreement
NGO	Non-Governmental Organisation
OECD	Organisation for Economic Co-operation and Development
UKTI	UK Trade & Investment
UNCTAD	United Nations Conference on Trade and Development
WAIPA	World Association of Investment Promotion Agencies
WEF	World Economic Forum
WTO	World Trade Organisation

Introduction

What a difference a few years can make. Only six years ago, the global economy seemed to be basking in a period of enduring prosperity. Investor confidence and activity was at an all-time high, emerging markets seemed to offer infinite possibilities, while developed economies, businesses and consumers rode the crest of a credit wave. When that wave broke up and came crashing on rocky shores in 2008, the world's economy entered a new paradigm, and the global Foreign Direct Investment (FDI) landscape was profoundly affected by this new paradigm – and in many ways.

As the two heat maps from fDi Markets in Figure I.1 illustrate, the geographical spread of leading FDI markets has narrowed considerably in the past few years. Up until the onset of the 2008 crisis, emerging markets such as Brazil, Russia, India and China (the four founding 'BRICS'), the Middle East and North Africa (MENA), as well as the US and numerous countries in Europe were the dominant destination countries in terms of capital investment flows. Since 2009, however, the landscape has been dominated by a smaller concentration of markets, with Russia and much of the MENA region in particular showing a lower degree of dominance. One commonly offered explanation for this shift is that corporations have predominantly sought stable operating environments for their investments in the wake of the crisis. A detailed analysis of investment flows and investor confidence in various markets will be given in Chapter 1, but these two maps are a revealing illustration of the various shifts that have taken place in the past few years.

FDI is one of the most talked-about areas of economic activity today, and the benefits it can bring are both important and numerous; here are just a few of them:

Figure I.1a   FDI destination market heat map – capital investment 2006–2008

Source: fDi Markets, www.fdimarkets.com.

Note: The darker the colour, the greater the relative level of capital investment.

Figure I.1b   FDI destination market heat map – capital investment 2009–2011

Source: fDi Markets, www.fdimarkets.com.

Note: The darker the colour, the greater the relative level of capital investment.

- **Job creation** – At a time when governments and other leaders are calling out for 'jobs, jobs and more jobs', FDI, unlike other forms of investment, typically leads not only to the creation of direct jobs, but indirect ones too.

- **Wage premium** – Foreign companies typically pay higher wages than domestic ones.

- **Catalyst effect** – FDI has the potential to raise a location's overall brand profile and to spur 'follow-the-leader' investment, as well as supply chain and cluster development.

- **Innovation and domestic investment** – FDI can intensify local market competition, thus creating the stimulus for innovation. It is also estimated that US$1 from FDI leads to US$1 in domestic investment.[1]

- **Technology transfer** – Multinational corporations are more R&D-intensive, and control much of global R&D and patenting. Foreign investment from these can therefore transfer important technological know-how to recipient markets.

- **Higher productivity** – Increased technology transfers through FDI can also lead to higher productivity levels.

With potential benefits such as these, it is perhaps unsurprising that around 10,000 economic development organisations and investment promotion agencies are now estimated to exist worldwide,[2] all dedicated to the development of their economies through the attraction and retention of FDI. At the same time, corporations are seeking to balance cautious optimism with the need for sustainable growth through new markets and cost efficiencies. Compare the number of economic development organisations globally with the average annual number of FDI projects worldwide over the past couple of years (a little over 13,000[3]), and the figures are pretty close. The result is a 'scramble' for investment on a global scale, and economic development organisations in particular are faced with a highly competitive environment where smart approaches to differentiation, engagement and investment services are becoming increasingly critical to success.

---

1   Estimate from the economic development consultancy OCO Global.
2   Ibid. The term economic development organisation (EDO) is typically used in North America, while investment promotion agency (IPA) is more commonplace elsewhere. In this book, the term economic development organisation will be used, and refers to both.
3   According to data from fDi Markets, there were 12,985 FDI projects globally in 2010 and 13,713 in 2011.

These strategic approaches don't only need to take on board this new investment paradigm; as the global landscape continues to evolve, they too will need to evolve and reflect the world in which we live. Predicting the future is of course a tricky, unreliable business – events over the past few years alone have made that clear – and yet there are five telling signs that I believe give a snapshot of how the global FDI landscape may be influenced over the next couple of decades.

BRAVE NEW WORLD...

1. By 2020, it's predicted that the founding BRIC markets could account for nearly 50 per cent of all global GDP growth.[4]

2. More than 50 per cent of African households are set to have discretionary spending power by 2020.[5]

3. By 2020, China will have an estimated 35.5 million students enrolled[6] – that's greater than the entire current population of Canada. In 2010 alone, India had around 50 foreign universities expressing an interest in setting up in the country; meanwhile, 96 per cent of the world's top 50 universities are currently in developed markets.[7]

4. Social networks are set to become the main form of business communication for 20 per cent of employees worldwide as early as 2014.[8]

5. Finally, clean technology (or 'clean tech') will increasingly drive both governmental and corporate growth agendas: 75 per cent of multinational corporations surveyed by Ernst & Young in 2010 expected their clean tech spending to increase by 2015.[9] Meanwhile, the International Energy Agency (IEA) recently predicted that power generation from renewable sources will triple between 2010 and 2035.[10]

---

4   *Tracking Global Trends: How Six Key Developments are Shaping the Business World*, Ernst & Young, 2011, p. 4.

5   *Lions on the Move: The Progress and Potential of African Economies*, McKinsey Global Institute, 2010, p. 4.

6   China's *Guidelines of the National Program for Educational Reform and Development* set out the country's goals in developing higher education.

7   According to the QS World University Rankings 2011/12, only two universities from emerging markets made the top 50 list: Peking University and Tsinghua University.

8   Prediction made by the global IT research firm Gartner in November 2010.

9   *Tracking Global Trends.*

10 *World Energy Outlook*, International Energy Agency, 2010, p. 5.

This book offers an exploration of some of the key trends, issues and practices that are shaping the global FDI landscape, and provides insight into how economic developers and investors alike can make the most of their opportunities and mitigate reputational and communications challenges that can impede or hinder a successful investment. What lessons have been learnt since the economic downturn which began in 2008? How can a location's brand act as a 'guarantor' of foreign investment? What protectionist developments are we witnessing in the FDI space, and how can corporations develop a better understanding of what drives these measures in order to address, counter or challenge them? And what about the perspectives of corporate investors? What factors matter to them, and where do economic developers therefore need to focus their efforts? International politics and public diplomacy can also have an important bearing on FDI, and we'll examine both the potential and limitations of governmental involvement. Finally, where is the global FDI landscape headed? What forces are shaping the way in which economic developers now need to present their offers and engage with investors?

Dubai: a city built on more than sand. The transformation of Dubai's architectural landscape over the past couple of decades is a key symbol of the city's rise from obscure desert community to regional metropolis and world-class city brand

Photo: © iStockphoto.com / Uwe Merkel

1 FDI in a Downturn: Trends and Lessons Learned

What we clearly need are new models for global, regional, national and business decision-making which truly reflect that the context for decision-making has been altered – in unprecedented ways.

Klaus Schwab

The keystone for all foreign direct investment is confidence, and the bedrock of confidence is stability. Ever since the 2007 subprime mortgage crisis heralded the onslaught of the worst global financial meltdown since the Great Depression, we have been living in a far more questioning – and far less confident – world.

It therefore came as no surprise that levels of global FDI activity declined in 2009 compared with 2007 and 2008.[1] FDI inflows saw a progressive decline from an all-time high of US$1.97 trillion in 2007 to just under US$1.2 trillion in 2009, based on figures from the United Nations Conference on Trade and Development (UNCTAD).[2] Since 2009, seen by many as having been the height of the crisis, there have been increasing signs of economic green shoots around the world, with a corresponding rise in international investment: as Figure 1.1 shows, 2010 saw inflows rise modestly to just under US$1.31 trillion, while the pace of recovery quickened slightly in 2011, which saw inflows rise by more than 16 per cent to just over US$1.52 trillion,[3] slightly above the pre-crisis average during 2005–2007.

---

1 According to fDi Markets' *Global Outlook Report 2010*, there was a 14 per cent decline in FDI projects in 2009 compared to 2008.
2 *World Investment Report 2012*, UNCTAD, July 2012, p. 169.
3 Ibid.

In spite of these promising signs, it would be far too optimistic to say that we are on the fast track to a full recovery. Ongoing concerns around double-dip recessions and uncertainties around the nature and speed of recovery in various countries and regions (referred to by many in the business and political worlds as the 'LUV'-shaped recovery[4]) mean that many would-be international investors are continuing to postpone investments until the macroeconomic situation becomes clearer and more stable.

A counterbalance to this cautious stance, however, is the perceived need among some companies to grow their businesses in new markets with lower costs and more dynamic consumption. Of those companies continuing to invest in this uncertain economic climate, access to new markets and capacity-building in preparation for the economic rebound are the two most important drivers of investment decisions, according to A.T. Kearney's 2010 FDI Confidence Index.[5] The firm's more recent 2012 Confidence Index found that more than a third of investors were increasing their investments in emerging markets.[6]

8

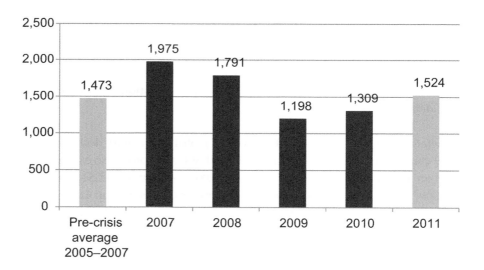

Figure 1.1   Global FDI flows, average 2005–2007 and 2007–2011
Source: World Investment Report 2012, UNCTAD

---

4   The 'LUV'-shaped recovery refers to the different types of recovery markets around the world have been displaying: either a swift recovery (V-shaped), a more gradual recovery (U-shaped), or in the worst-case scenario, a prolonged economic slump (L-shaped).
5   *Investing in a Rebound: The 2010 FDI Confidence Index*, A.T. Kearney, 2010, p. 4.
6   *Cautious Investors Feed a Tentative Recovery: The 2012 A.T. Kearney FDI Confidence Index*, A.T. Kearney, November 2011, p. 10.

This first chapter examines those locations around the world that now inspire confidence among investors, as well as those erstwhile FDI hotspots which have now fallen out of favour with the international investment community, and ultimately seeks to shed light on the reasons behind their respective successes and declines.

ASIA CONTINUES TO STEAM AHEAD

In broad terms, the Asia-Pacific region seems to have been at the forefront of investors' minds over the past few years. Market research conducted by fDi Intelligence in early 2010 indicated that Asia-Pacific was the top destination region in 2009, while in A.T. Kearney's 2010 FDI Confidence Index, 72 per cent of respondents believed that the region would lead the world out of recession.[7] Two of the top three markets in the firm's 2012 index are also from Asia-Pacific – unsurprisingly, these are the region's two economic powerhouses, China and India, which came in first and second place respectively.

The leadership of China and India when it comes to investor interest and FDI flows is likely to continue unabated for the foreseeable future; their market potential as the world's two distinctly most populated countries, coupled with their ongoing investments in infrastructure, higher education and a host of other FDI attributes, will ensure that they not only remain major FDI targets (that is, 'host economies'), but will also increasingly become sources of FDI (or 'home economies'). China was the second largest recipient of FDI in 2009, and by 2011 featured among the top five investors in the world.[8]

There has been much speculation over where the world's most populous country and second global economy is headed over the next couple of decades, and what this will entail for FDI. Some statistics have pointed to a potential slowing down of FDI into China – for example, at the end of 2011, inflows declined by 9.7 per cent in November and 12.7 per cent in December, according to China's Ministry of Commerce,[9] and with rising wages and costs, questions are increasingly being raised around the country's long-term prospects for cost-saving FDI. This is only one small part of the broader FDI perspective, however, and for those investors seeking access to China's vast and rapidly urbanising consumer markets, those rising wages are not an impediment, but rather an opportunity. And that opportunity is immense, stretching far beyond the well-known cities and provinces on China's coast

---

7   *Investing in a Rebound*, p. 6.
8   *World Investment Report 2011*, UNCTAD, July 2011, p. 9. Hong Kong, meanwhile, was the fourth largest source market for FDI in 2011.
9   As reported in 'Foreign Investment into China Slows', *Forbes*, 19 January 2012.

(Shanghai, Guangzhou, Hong Kong and so on). The Economist Intelligence Unit (EIU) pointed out in its recent report on FDI into China that a major westerly shift was taking place within the country: in 2007, the south-western city of Chongqing ranked just twenty-second out of China's 31 provinces for FDI, but by 2011, it had overtaken the capital, Beijing.[10]

India's prospects are also extremely bright as a foreign investment location. While it went from second to third place in A.T. Kearney's 2010 Confidence Index (swapping places with the United States), it reclaimed second position in the company's 2012 index[11] (while the US moved down to fourth place). India featured among the top ten host economies in 2009, attracting US$35.6 billion of FDI inflows,[12] and while the country's inflows fell dramatically in 2010 to US$24.2 billion,[13] 2011 saw a significant upturn, with investment levels rising by more than 30 per cent to US$31.6 billion.[14] The legacy of the 2010 Commonwealth Games, hosted by Delhi, is sadly likely to remain somewhat tainted by those shocking images of that collapsed footbridge and the insalubrious bathrooms and stray dogs on beds in the athlete's village. Stories and images such as these carry great potency and tend to engender implications far beyond the realities behind them. Perception is reality, as the old maxim goes. And yet India's realities have the potential to portray a far more promising image of a country which is the world's largest democracy and whose rate of growth could possibly overtake that of China within the next few years. India's innovative and entrepreneurial attributes are numerous and impressive: the country has pioneered the US$2,000 car and affordable surgery, while its major corporations are truly global players with business empires that stretch well beyond India's borders. Such innovation and entrepreneurialism benefit not only India's outward investment, but are also major inward investment attributes as the global economy becomes more knowledge-intensive.

BRITANNIA NO LONGER RULES THE WAVES (BUT HOPEFULLY THE UK CAN CONTINUE TO RIDE THEM)

The upward trends being witnessed in China and India – whose inflows started picking up as early as mid-2009 – contrast starkly with those being witnessed in much of the developed world. Investor confidence in the United Kingdom is reported to have fallen significantly since the crisis

---

10 *Serve the People: The New Landscape of Foreign Investment into China,* Economist Intelligence Unit, January 2012.
11 *Cautious Investors Feed a Tentative Recovery.*
12 *World Investment Report 2010.*
13 *World Investment Report 2012.*
14 Ibid.

began (from fourth place in 2007 to tenth place in 2010, recovering slightly to eighth place in 2012).[15] This overall decline in confidence over the past five years is reflected in the country's disappointing FDI inflows, which shrank by 50 per cent during 2008–2009, only to fall a further 35 per cent in 2010, although 2011 did see a modest rebound of 7 per cent.[16] Meanwhile, the decline in the country's profile as an international investor was even starker following the onset of the crisis (with outflows falling from US$161 billion in 2008 to just US$44 billion in 2009, while by 2010 they had shrunk even more to US$39 billion, which was roughly on par with Spain's outward FDI flows and lower than those of far smaller European economies like the Netherlands, Belgium and Switzerland).

This mixed five-year picture of FDI confidence and activity in the UK can be attributed to a number of factors, not least the fact that it was one of the first countries to fall victim to the financial crisis which exploded in late 2008. The UK economy's heavy dependence on the financial services industry exposed the country more than many to the turbulence of what was, with few exceptions, a global crisis. Investor confidence in the City of London slumped, and as the British government came in to prop up the banks and subsequently introduce legislation that would rein in the activities of investment banks and other financial actors, investors started questioning the future ease of doing business in a country which for more than a century has been seen as a bastion of the free market economy. The country had furthermore been in election mode ever since Gordon Brown pondered calling an election in the autumn of 2007. His decision not to proceed with an election that year, followed by the onset of the financial crisis in 2008, generated a long-lasting sentiment that an election was just around the corner (it was due to be held by May 2010 at the latest), and would strongly reflect the British people's judgement on how the government had handled the economic crisis. By late 2009, a landslide victory for David Cameron's Conservative Party was appearing increasingly unlikely, and prospects for a hung parliament – never an investment attribute – seemed increasingly feasible.

The UK's heavy dependence on the rest of Europe for trade is another part of the story, and to some extent explains why it has performed much worse on the FDI front than, say, the United States, which was also particularly hard hit by the recession and which we'll come to later. Investors in Europe have been far more reticent than those in other parts of the world over the past few years; A.T. Kearney's 2010 index revealed that 62 per cent of European companies were planning to postpone investments, compared with just

---

15 *Cautious Investors Feed a Tentative Recovery.*

16 All data from *World Investment Reports 2010, 2011* and *2012.*

46 per cent in North America and 42 per cent in Asia-Pacific.[17] The economic crises that have beset Greece, Spain and smaller economies like Latvia, Ireland and Hungary have done nothing to boost investor confidence in Europe either, and on the contrary have had serious repercussions across the Continent (including in the City and other financial centres). When it comes to preferred locations among European investors, A.T. Kearney's 2010 report found that the UK did not even figure among the top ten countries (while other major European economies like Germany, Italy and France all did).[18] However, as the country's economy begins to show signs of recovery and the UK coalition government continues to tackle the budget deficit, there's hope that investor confidence – and activity – in the country will begin to grow once more.

The effects of the economic downturn have reminded us that geography is key, as are the strategic partnerships which countries, regions, cities and companies alike forge to leverage their geographic advantages. If your neighbours are doing well, then you should fully leverage this to your advantage, as research suggests that companies prefer to invest closer to home.[19] If they're not doing so well, this may on the one hand give your country a competitive advantage within that region. However, you should also consider whether regional investors will have the appetite or confidence to invest abroad, and you might need to consider looking at other regions where economic prospects are brighter and investor confidence is higher.

RUSSIA: THE UNDERPERFORMING BRIC?

The sluggish economic growth we're currently seeing across much of Europe is one of the core factors behind the disappointing levels of investor confidence and activity not only in developed European countries, but even in major emerging markets like Russia, where FDI inflows dropped from US$75 billion in 2008 to just US$36.5 billion in 2009 – the greatest drop of all the founding BRIC markets.[20] Flows have since started to recover, reaching US$43 billion in 2010 and rising to just under US$53 billion in 2011.[21] The gap compared to pre-crisis levels therefore remains significant.

The wavering levels of FDI inflows to Russia over the past few years can arguably be attributed to various factors – some of which are regional and

---

17 *Investing in a Rebound*, p. 5.
18 Ibid. p. 6.
19 Ibid. A.T. Kearney's data showed that investors from Asia-Pacific, Europe and North America demonstrate a preference for near abroad locations.
20 *World Investment Report 2012*, p. 172.
21 Ibid.

even global, while others are national. A slump in cross-border merger and acquisitions (M&A) activity by European firms, coupled with a drop in demand at home, were prime contributors to the initial decline, and yet Russia's importance as a source and target of investment remains high – it ranked eighth in UNCTAD's lists of both host and home economies in 2010.[22] It was also the first of the BRIC countries to become a net outward investor.

While these economic figures portray a relatively sound picture of a country which has seemingly held its ground in the midst of the global economic downturn, investor confidence indicators evoke questions about future investment perspectives for Russia, and whether the country is underperforming in relation to its investment potential as Europe's most populous country and one of the world's richest in terms of natural resources. In A.T. Kearney's 2007 Investor Confidence Index, Russia came in ninth place; in the 2010 index, it slumped to eighteenth place, but has since regained at least some ground, coming in at twelfth place in the 2012 index.

13

So what has been behind this mixed performance over the past few years? Firstly, Russia's economic downturn during the global crisis was far more severe than the other BRIC countries.[23] Secondly, high-profile stories of would-be investors like IKEA halting their projects drew attention to concerns they and other multinationals have about alleged corruption in Russia and its impact on their businesses. Then there are more sinister and politically charged stories which, while not investment-related, nevertheless evoked concern among a wide variety of international stakeholders with an interest in Russia (including business leaders). Take the case of the British Council in Russia as one example. In January 2008, the UK cultural organisation's employees were called in for interviews by Russia's security service, and some were visited by Interior Ministry officials at their homes late one evening. Furthermore, the head of the British Council's St Petersburg office, Stephen Kinnock, was detained and accused of drink-driving. These moves were seen by the British authorities and media as a campaign of intimidation, firstly against an organisation which had had long-standing disputes with the Russian authorities regarding its tax status, and secondly against the UK government, with which Russia had been in tense diplomatic relations following the death of former KGB agent Alexander Litvinenko.[24]

---

22 *World Investment Report 2011*, pp. 4 and 9.
23 Russia's GDP growth declined from 5.2 per cent in 2008 to -7.9 per cent in 2009, according to the International Monetary Fund's World Economic Outlook Database. In contrast, China's growth rate only declined from 9.5 per cent to 9 per cent and India's from 6.4 per cent to 5.7 per cent in the same period. Brazil's declined from 5.1 per cent to −0.2 per cent.
24 'Russia Warned Over "Intimidation"', http://news.bbc.co.uk/1/hi/uk_politics/7191411. stm, 16 January 2008 (accessed 9 July 2012).

International investors, like all people, ultimately want to feel comfortable in the country where they live, and have the often challenging task of persuading their top executives (and their families) to relocate to these countries. Stories like that of the British Council in Russia therefore carry significant weight, and they're not easily forgotten.

While this controversy is unlikely to have had any adverse impact on overall investment flows, stories such as these can – in sufficient quantity, regularity and gravity – significantly contribute to investors' opinions about a place, thus leading them to go beyond classic considerations of short- to medium-term return on investment and consider wider issues such as financial and personal risks and their company's reputation.

Yet there have been some positive recent developments that point to brighter FDI prospects for Russia. At the end of 2011, the country formally joined the World Trade Organisation – a move hailed by numerous Western leaders as an important step towards further integrating Russia with the international community. This optimism is reflected in investor confidence, with Russia moving up to twelfth place in the 2012 A.T. Kearney index from eighteenth place in 2007,[25] as well as in some key high-profile investments such as PepsiCo's US$3.8 billion acquisition of the food and drink brand Wimm-Bill-Dann and ExxonMobil's joint venture with Rosneft in August 2011. This latter case arguably displayed an important degree of confidence in the country's investment climate, considering the major difficulties BP had encountered in its attempts to forge a partnership with the Russian oil company only earlier that year – a case which will be examined in greater detail in Chapter 5.

THE EUROPEAN PARADOX

Heading west, much of Europe has been embroiled in the ongoing eurozone crisis over the past few years. For the first time since the crisis began, references have been made to Greece as the 'Lehman Brothers' of European states, although thus far at least, Greece, like so many of the similarly troubled banks, has been deemed 'too big to fail'. The political will demonstrated through the massive bailouts has to some degree sent a strong signal to governments and investors around the world that not only is Greece too big to fail, but so too is the eurozone, and implicitly, the European Union itself.

---

25 *Cautious Investors Feed a Tentative Recovery.*

Paradoxically, much of Europe has seen some positive developments on the FDI front, in spite of the macroeconomic woes besieging the eurozone. FDI flows into Europe overall grew by 19 per cent in 2011 to US$425 billion, while certain countries like Austria, Portugal and Italy saw far higher increases in inflows.[26] While much of these European inflows can be attributed to an increase in cross-border M&A activity as corporations have sought to restructure and stabilise their operations in the wake of the crisis, overall confidence levels in many of Europe's major economies appear at least to be stabilising, and in some cases improving. Germany, the eurozone's largest economy, retained its position in fifth place in A.T. Kearney's 2012 FDI Confidence Index, while the UK, Switzerland, Spain and the Netherlands all rose in the ranking compared with 2010. France and Poland also remain on the top 25 list, even though the latter fell substantially from sixth place in 2010 to twenty-third place in 2012. While this drop seems disappointing, it should be seen in the context of Poland's extraordinary resilience throughout the downturn years, which arguably tilted FDI confidence disproportionately in its favour while other European economies suffered.

THE EUROPEAN UNION AS GUARANTOR AND ROLE MODEL?

In spite of Europe's ongoing troubles, strong and effective structures of governance offered by the EU nevertheless play an important role. Over and above being part of the world's largest and most integrated economic bloc, accession to the EU brings a host of other investment attributes – for host country and investors alike. Accession first and foremost gives a country a 'golden seal of approval' from Brussels and all the other EU capitals – it represents the fulfilment of a very extensive and stringent set of governance criteria (known as the Copenhagen Criteria) which range from political stability and the maintenance of a free market economy to the rule of law to anti-corruption measures and civil liberties.[27]

Critics will of course point to the recent economic troubles that have engulfed not only Greece, but Ireland, Italy, Portugal and Spain as well. Far from bestowing 'golden seals of approval', they will argue that the EU and its 'eurocrats' in Brussels turned a blind eye to economic mismanagement in these countries' respective capitals. To an extent this is a valid argument, and yet it overlooks the fact that the economic criteria are now being much

---

26 *World Investment Report 2012*. Inflows increased by 228 per cent in Austria, 215 per cent in Italy and 296 per cent in Portugal.

27 A detailed description of the Copenhagen Criteria may be found on the EU's 'EUROPA' web portal: http://europa.eu/scadplus/glossary/accession_criteria_copenhague_en.htm (accessed 9 July 2012).

more stringently applied and monitored. It is almost certainly too late to talk of EU and eurozone membership having granted a credible economic 'clean bill of health' for Greece, and similarly there are valid theoretical questions over whether countries like Spain, Italy and Portugal would have been admitted to the eurozone if the economic criteria had been applied more vigorously when assessing the state of their public finances. However, the fact remains that the eurozone – for all its current woes – remains an investment attribute, enabling international investors to operate far more freely and easily across its 17 member states than when each of these had their own separate currencies.

Beyond the specific concerns around the euro, the EU actually has a highly sophisticated ecosystem of checks and balances in place. When corporate concerns, grievances and disputes arise, there are a host of institutions – from the European Commission and Parliament to the European Court of Justice (ECJ) – all on hand to act as the guardians of the *Acquis Communautaire* (the EU's set of laws) and to protect the EU's four fundamental freedoms – the free movement of goods, people, services and capital.

The confidence which economic integration and monetary union inspire has led blocs elsewhere to follow in the EU's footsteps – take the countries of East Africa as a prime example. We will explore Africa's investment landscape and potential later on in this chapter, but it is worth making a brief reference here to the East African Community (EAC), as the rapid process of integration has been an important contributor to the EAC's emergence as one of the continent's key emerging powerhouses. With monetary union (the East African shilling) scheduled for 2015 at the time of writing, and full political union into a single East African Federation thereafter[28] – Kenya, Uganda and Tanzania have not only followed in the EU's footsteps, they're potentially about to leapfrog it, and with FDI inflows showing continued overall growth,[29] signs point to a highly promising investment climate for the region.

LATIN AMERICA'S DECADE

Latin America provides another example of successful economic integration among emerging markets in the form of the Southern Common Market

---

28 South Sudan's recent potential accession talks with the EAC mean that a concrete timeframe for the creation of a federation remained unclear at the time of writing.

29 According to UNCTAD's 2012 figures, inflows into Kenya rose from US$116 million in 2009 to US$335 million in 2011; in Tanzania, they rose more modestly from US$953 million in 2009 to just under US$1.1 billion in 2011.

(Mercosur) and the recently created Community of Latin American and Caribbean Countries (CELAC). In 2012, the region's economic powerhouse, Brazil, was the third most attractive FDI destination market globally, according to A.T. Kearney (up from fourth place in 2010 and sixth place in 2007), and while FDI inflows into the country fell by 42 per cent during 2008–2009 (a greater decline than the region as a whole[30]), the figures from 2010 and 2011 show a that an encouraging recovery has since been under way[31] and that prospects for Brazil's future as an FDI source and target country are very bright – on a variety of fronts. The country's traditional strengths in agriculture and commodities look set to grow, with major inward investments such as those from BG Group, the British energy company, which plans to invest US$20 billion in Brazil over the next ten years. Meanwhile, Brazil's profile as an industrial heavyweight and international investor was given a significant boost in September 2010 when the country's oil giant Petrobras raised a record-breaking US$70 billion, setting a new record as the world's largest initial public offering (IPO) and helping the company to fund what is expected to become one of the world's largest oil exploration plans to date.[32]

Yet it is more than energy and other natural resources that are fuelling growth and investor confidence in Brazil. The coming decade will see the country host two world-class sporting events – the FIFA World Cup in 2014 and the Summer Olympics in 2016. Such events put their hosts in the global spotlight and present the city or country with an opportunity to showcase their attributes to a worldwide audience not only of sporting fans, but also politicians, tourists, business leaders, and therefore would-be investors. Brazil is already seeing growing interest in its consumer, retail and fast-moving consumer goods (FMCG) sectors. Coca-Cola announced it would increase its investments in Brazil by 75 per cent during 2010–2015, while Wal-Mart bucked the investment trend by investing a third more in Brazil in 2009 than it did in 2008.[33] Brazil has it all to play for in the coming years – quite literally. The onus is now on the Brazilian government and its partners to harness the enthusiasm and passion of a people where sport (and football in particular) is an institution. These games present far more than moments of national pride and opportunities to dominate the world's media for a couple of months. With a well-planned strategy to complement them, these events provide an opportunity to drive innovation and productivity among

---

30 *World Investment Report 2010*; FDI in Latin America and the Caribbean stood at US$117 billion in 2009 – down 36 per cent on 2008 levels.

31 *World Investment Report 2012*; inflows into Brazil rose by 37.5 per cent during 2010–11.

32 'Petrobras to Sell $65 Billion Stock in Record Offer', Brian Ellsworth, Reuters, http://www.reuters.com/article/idUSTRE6821FX20100903, 3 September 2010 (accessed 9 July 2012).

33 *Investing in a Rebound*, p. 16.

Brazil's workforce and emerging talent, showcasing the country's potential to investors around the world.

While Brazil may be the focus of many international headlines, other economies in the region are demonstrating similar and even greater developments in FDI attraction. Colombia, for example, saw the greatest regional increase in FDI inflows during 2010–2011, rising by an impressive 91 per cent from US$6.9 billion in 2010 to US$13.2 billion in 2011.[34] Chile, meanwhile, is broadly regarded as one of the region's most open economies, with 16 free trade agreements (FTAs) in place, and often leads the region in various business rankings and indices such as the World Economic Forum's *Global Competitiveness Report*, the World Bank's *Ease of Doing Business* and the Heritage Foundation's *Economic Freedom Index*. These attributes have helped the country attract increasing levels of FDI over the past few years, rising from $US12.9 billion in 2009[35] to 17.3 billion in 2011.

Further north, Mexico has traditionally been another major contributor to the region's rise to prominence. As one of the 'Next 11' (N11), Mexico continues attract significant levels of FDI (second only in the region to Brazil), in spite of poor macroeconomic performance in 2009, when it saw its GDP contract by 7.1 per cent (the worse the country had seen in more than seventy years). Inflows did drop slightly by 5.3 per cent however during 2010–2011, from US$20.7 billion to US$19.6 billion. Investor confidence, meanwhile, has recently seen a more substantial slump: Mexico fell off A.T. Kearney's 2012 Confidence Index, having previously climbed from nineteenth position in 2007 up to eighth position in 2010.[36] This slump in confidence can to a large extent be explained by the country's ongoing instabilities and violence, fuelled by wars between the country's numerous drugs cartels which have received significant international media coverage. Much of Mexico's fortunes also depend on its northern neighbour and fellow NAFTA member, the United States, and just as the latter's economic troubles during the crisis resulted in plummeting levels of FDI for Mexico, so too will the USA's projected economic recovery play a large part in Mexico's future investment prospects, as US firms wary of domestic tax conditions and heightened costs seek to make savings by near-shoring[37] their operations across the southern border. However, experience has shown time and again that it is never advisable to be overdependent on one industry or

---

34 *World Investment Report 2012.*
35 Ibid.
36 Ibid.
37 'Near-shoring' is defined by the business outsourcing magazine *SourcingMag.com* as: 'the transfer of business or IT processes to companies in a nearby country, often sharing a border with your own country'.

trade partner, especially given Barack Obama's recent calls and proposed incentives for US firms to invest domestically by 'onshoring' rather than off-shoring or near-shoring. As such, investments such as La Caixa's 20 per cent stake in Grupo Financiero Imbrusa are a welcome indicator of Mexico's strong ties with other parts of the world. The country's profile as an international investor is also on the rise, with home-grown companies such as CEMEX continuing to expand their operations internationally in regions that previously had little in the way of socio-political or economic connections with Mexico, such as Central and South East Europe.

TRIUMPH IN THE FACE OF ADVERSITY

With the notable exception of parts of Europe, many of the examples covered so far have by and large seen correlations between the macroeconomic situation or dynamism of the country or the region and the levels of investment and investor confidence they attract. Relative stability and sustained growth amidst the economic crisis (or at least promising signs of recovery) have generally been rewarded with relatively sustained levels of investor confidence and a less stark drop in investor activity, while markets that have been more severely hit by recession have seen FDI activity and investor confidence either stagnate, or worse still, slump. Two exceptions to this trend come to mind, however – the United States and Dubai. Both have very different stories, and yet both cases reveal a number of trends and truths that arguably have important leanings for destinations around the world.

Prior to the onset of the economic downturn, both the USA and Dubai appeared to represent the embodiment of consumer and corporate confidence, where commercial and residential real estate development continued to boom. In Dubai, progress on the construction of the world's tallest building, the Burj Dubai (later renamed the Burj Khalifa), became a potent symbol of the emirate's confidence and boldness – a land of superlatives where you can sunbathe on the Jumeirah beach in the afternoon, then head off to the Mall of the Emirates for a skiing session on the slopes (with real snow!) in the evening. In the USA, consumer confidence and easy access to credit continued to propel the economy to dizzying heights.

Then the US subprime mortgage crisis exploded onto the scene and changed everything. Images of empty newly built homes and swimming pools with stagnant, murky green-coloured water became iconic symbols in newspapers and on TV, both in the USA and around the world. Consumer confidence began to falter, and it soon became devastatingly clear that the situation would get far worse before it got any better. By late 2008, Dubai's numerous cranes had by and large come to a standstill and increasing turbulence in the global financial marketplace heralded stormier weather to come.

The images and stories that came to portray the Dubai and US economies between late 2008 and mid-2010 certainly highlighted the degree to which they fell victim to the global economic crisis. Massive bailouts from the federal capitals – whether they were from Washington, DC, or in the case of Dubai, from their richer neighbouring emirate and UAE capital, Abu Dhabi – appear to have spelled an abrupt end to an era of flamboyant spending.

And yet the recent cases of the USA and Dubai are far from negative ones when it comes to investor confidence and attracting FDI. For all its financial woes, the USA has broadly held its ground when it comes to foreign investor confidence (it moved up from third place in A.T. Kearney's 2007 FDI Confidence Index to second place in 2010, and while it fell to fourth place in 2012, it still remained the top developed country on the list). Inflows also rose in 2008 to US$306 billion (up from US$216 billion in 2007), and while they subsequently saw a decline to US$144 billion in 2009 as the crisis took hold, they have since made an encouraging recovery (standing at US$227 billion in 2011).[38] Yet while there's cause for optimism, there's no room for complacency. Barack Obama has recently spoken of the need for the USA to up its game on what is seen as the country's unfulfilled FDI potential and explains the US administration's recent decision to expand the country's recently formed national FDI agency, SelectUSA.[39]

Meanwhile, the UAE remains the number one investment location in the Middle East – a region which saw foreign investment soar from just US$3 billion in 2000 to US$78 billion by 2008.[40] The country remained on A.T. Kearney's 2012 Confidence Index in fifteenth place – an achievement, given the recent instabilities in the broader MENA region. Within the UAE, Dubai is the clear leader when it comes to investor confidence, with 28 per cent of investors surveyed by A.T. Kearney in 2010 citing the emirate as their preferred choice for future investment (followed by 18 per cent for neighbouring Abu Dhabi).[41] More impressively, 81 per cent of respondents with investments in Dubai intended to maintain or raise the level of their investments in the emirate in the coming years, in spite of all the negative publicity it has received in recent times. Such investor confidence and interest cannot be attributed to one or a couple of factors; the reality is that a myriad

---

38 *World Investment Report 2012.*

39 At the beginning of 2012 it was announced that SelectUSA would have a proposed budget of US$13 million in 2013 to proactively assist economic growth and job creation at the federal level.

40 *Investing in a Rebound,* p. 11.

41 Ibid.

of attributes – both tangible and intangible – contribute to Dubai's unrivalled attractiveness as an investment location in the Middle East.

Let's start with the tangible attributes – and infrastructure has certainly been an important part of Dubai's success story, both within the city and though its regionally unrivalled network of flight routes to the rest of the world. Dubai has long been, and appears set to remain, the gateway not only to the Gulf, but to the wider Middle East, East and Southern Africa and South-West Asia, helped to some degree by the fact that it is broadly reachable by plane within eight hours or less from almost all major cities in Europe, Asia-Pacific and Africa. Dubai's free zones have also have been key to the emirate's success as an investment hub. Furthermore, investors also cite ease of doing business and the emirate's safe environment as important considerations.[42] Meanwhile, the recent instabilities in the broader MENA region might be seen as a double-edged sword; on the one hand, investors using Dubai as a platform to gain access to the wider region will now be more reticent than before the Arab Spring, while on the other, the emirate now offers a distinctly safe investor haven in an otherwise unstable and unpredictable region.

So what about the intangible attributes, like Dubai's reputation, and ultimately, its brand? The importance of a place's brand in attracting FDI and suggested approaches for optimising a place's brand are topics we will explore in greater depth in Chapter 2, but this is a suitable moment to make a reference to the brands of Dubai and the United States, as in both cases they have arguably been one of the key contributing factors to their continuing successes as sources and targets of FDI.

DUBAI: A CITY BUILT ON MORE THAN SAND

Compare images of Dubai in the early 1990s with those of the city today and it's striking how much the city has grown in such a short space of time. Dubai's story is undoubtedly one of boldness and – to a degree – audacity. It is quite literally a futuristic metropolis built on sand, yet unlike the infamous parable of the foolish man who built his house upon sand, Dubai's model has proven to be not only sustainable, but also an inspiration, to the extent that other cities in the Gulf and even further afield are now seeking to position themselves as 'the next Dubai'.

Dubai's iconic architecture, infrastructure, ease of doing business, Western-friendly outlook and impressive leisure amenities have all contributed to the creation of a powerful place brand that has attracted investment from across

---

42 The UAE is one of the few countries in the Middle East not to have fallen victim to a single act of terrorism by Al Qaeda or other terrorist groups since 2001.

the globe and has inspired hundreds of thousands of executives and their families to relocate. If ever there was a city which followed and reaped the rewards of that old maxim 'build it and they will come', it's Dubai.

AMERICA: THE 'DOYEN' OF PLACE BRANDS

If Dubai is the epitome of 'the wonder that came from nowhere', then the United States, our other FDI success story, is the grand old veteran of place brands whose world-leading position arguably remains unchallenged to this day – even in a world of seismic geopolitical and macroeconomic shifts. The country itself and its major corporations certainly face unprecedented competition globally, and it is certainly true that globalisation and 'Americanisation' are no longer synonymous. That said, 'Brand America' and its multitude of components continue to dominate the global commercial and cultural landscape – from US corporate behemoths and the millions of foreign workers they employ in their overseas operations to Hollywood blockbusters to Lady Gaga and Facebook.

So why does all this matter for investment? In essence, a brand – whether we're talking about a product, a company or a place – is that entity's licence to operate; it's their reputation. Just as a good reputation helps to inspire confidence – be it from a consumer, an employee, a tourist or an investor – a bad reputation hinders or erodes confidence, and thus interaction. Therefore, when it comes to attracting FDI, cities, regions and nations need to consider how their place brand is portrayed and communicated to the outside world through various channels and stakeholders, and we will examine how place brands and reputations are built and sustained in greater detail in Chapter 2. In the same vein, foreign investors and export promotion bodies need to ask similar questions about their country of origin's brand in order to leverage or detract from that brand image as appropriate. For all its controversial engagements around the world – past and present, commercial, political and military – 'Brand America' continues to play its part in helping the United States to attract far greater FDI inflows than any other world economy. It has also helped to broadly sustain investor confidence in the country.

The United States and Dubai are two examples of how familiarity drives favourability. Other examples later in this book will illustrate how the opposite also tends to be true, and that a lack of transparency, visibility and profiling internationally can impede or, worse still, scupper efforts to invest or attract investment. Likewise, reputation-building efforts not grounded in reality will either fail from the outset, or at best have a limited shelf life. With one audacious project following another, many did question whether Dubai's vision and resulting reputation-building efforts were indeed grounded in reality, or rather whether they were shaky dreams built on sand. There have been failures along the way that have fuelled such questioning, such as 'The World' construction project which virtually (not literally!) ran aground in late 2009. Other projects may turn out to be nothing more than pipedreams, or grandiose designs, artists' impressions and models that adorn exhibition centres, flashy interactive websites and glossy promotional collateral, but never actually become a reality. And yet Dubai *is* grounded in reality, *living* the dream, and proving that in the space of less than two decades you can build a world-class city capable of competing with those that have been international commercial hubs for centuries.

A NEW 'SCRAMBLE' FOR AFRICA

The one outstanding continent this chapter has not yet covered is the very continent that's increasingly at the forefront of investors' minds when considering where opportunities lie if not in the immediate term then certainly in the medium to long term. As those who seek to invest abroad and attract FDI face an unprecedented 'scramble' in an ever more crowded, interconnected and competitive world, nowhere is this scramble becoming more evident than in Africa. The term 'scramble', specifically with regard to Africa, is clearly charged with historical (namely colonial) significance, and it is not a coincidence that I refer to a new scramble for Africa here and elsewhere in this book. Chapter 3 will further explore this term within the context of what is sometimes regarded – rightly or wrongly – as 'neo-imperialistic' or 'hostile' foreign investment, but for now, let us take a brief at look at broader reasons behind this emerging investor interest in Africa.

Winston Churchill famously claimed that 'statistics are like a drunk with a lamppost: used more for support than illumination'. When it comes to summarising the development of a place like Africa, however, I would argue that statistics, used in the right context, *are* indeed illuminating and shed light on what is happening to a place with a degree of succinct clarity that other approaches often struggle to emulate. In 2008, Africa's collective GDP stood at US$1.6 trillion (roughly equal to Brazil's or Russia's) – by 2020, it is expected to grow to US$2.6 trillion. This projected GDP growth rate is far higher than the continent's projected population growth rate, as Figure 1.2 illustrates. UN statistics put Africa's current population at just over 1 billion. By 2020, it is predicted to rise to over 1.27 billion – nearly twice that of Europe's. Add to that a projection from McKinsey that more than 50 per cent of African households will have discretionary spending power by 2020,[43] and the continent's promise and potential are clear.

---

43 *Lions on the Move*, p. 4.

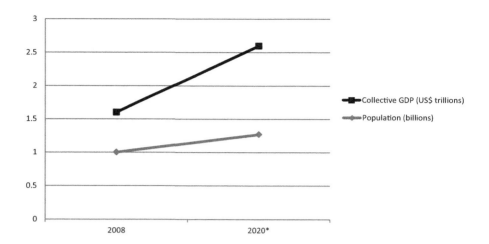

Figure 1.2   Africa's GDP growth far exceeds population growth
Sources: McKinsey Global Institute and the UN Population Division, 2010.
*   Predictions.

These macroeconomic statistics paint a positive picture for a continent that has long been (and still largely is) portrayed as a charity case – a reputational disconnect that will be addressed in Chapter 2. When it comes to attracting FDI, however, Africa is still some way off fulfilling its potential. During 2008–2009, FDI inflows fell by 9 per cent to US$53 billion (largely as a result of a decline in global commodity prices during the economic downturn). Matters did not improve after the worst of the crisis had passed, either: in 2010, inflows fell further to US$43.1 billion, followed by a more modest decline of just over 1 per cent in 2011, falling to US$42.6 billion.[44] In many ways, these successive declines are not surprising given the recent instabilities, particularly in North Africa. South Africa, however, has seen some more positive developments in recent years, with inflows jumping an impressive 373 per cent during 2010–2011. There are also signs that investor confidence in the country has rebounded – for example, it is the only African country to feature in A.T. Kearney's 2012 index, in eleventh position.[45]

So where next for Africa? The continent clearly has a number of emerging economic hotspots, from Kenya, Nigeria and Angola to more long-standing economic hubs like South Africa, now a member of the BRICS. Can the continent, its 53 countries and their multitude of stakeholders build on the learning and successes of other countries and regions around the world when it comes to attracting foreign investment and helping to enable African

---

44 *World Investment Report 2012.*
45 *Cautious Investors Feed a Tentative Recovery.*

companies to invest abroad? How can any place's brand (and thus reputation) be differentiated, built and sustained to attract FDI activity and investor confidence? The FDI successes and disappointments of the past few years have served as a powerful reminder of the critical role place brands, reputation-building and reputation management have to play.

Egypt and the Tahrir Square protests: Land of disorder or democratic awakening? While short-term FDI prospects have been dampened by Egypt's revolution, there are hopes that the youthful, tech-savvy country will garner significant investor interest in the longer term
Photo: Marwa Sameer Morgan

2

Place Brands: 'Guarantors' of Investment

Your premium brand had better be delivering something special, otherwise it's not going to get the business.

Warren Buffett

WHAT DO WE MEAN BY A BRAND?

The terms 'brand' and 'branding' have many meanings and are used by different groups in different ways. For non-marketers, 'brand' is often used to denote little more than the audio-visual representation of a product, a company or a place: its logo, tagline, theme-tune and so on. Meanwhile, 'branding' is taken to mean the practice of designing and developing these audio-visual elements for use in marketing campaigns. While these activities all have their rightful place in the brand mix, they have come to symbolise an attribute and a discipline which are in fact far broader than this – and these interpretations matter. At a recent investment conference I attended in Egypt, a delegate remarked as we went into a session on 'Branding Africa' that if he had to sit through a presentation and panel discussion on the development of 'yet another logo and tagline', then he would leave the conference early for a siesta at his nearby hotel. Fortunately for him and the other delegates, this was not the focus of the session, which instead explored greater questions and issues relating to Africa's reputation.

Reputation, as I indicated in Chapter 1, is the angle through which I will look at place brands when it comes to attracting and promoting FDI. A well-designed logo and catchy tagline integrated into an effective advertising campaign may certainly appeal to open-minded tourists and encourage them to find out more about a place before deciding where to travel. Investors, on the other hand, will not be attracted to a place in the same way, as their stakes are so much higher. To attract investors, a place's reputation matters greatly, and reputations are fundamentally complex and multifaceted.

NO SILVER BULLET, BUT GOLDEN RULES

There is no silver bullet for optimum place reputation management, because the reputation's composite elements and stakeholders are as diverse as they are numerous. However, there are a number of truths and golden rules for reputation-building and reputation management that have been proven to help optimise place brands and attract investment:

- **Authenticity is key** – A marketing and communications campaign which is not grounded in reality will ultimately fail. Stories and messages need to be authentic, and potential issues must be addressed through deeds as much as words. FDI projects, by their sheer size and longevity, tend to carefully considered, well-researched undertakings, and it isn't hard for would-be investors to gain a broad, detailed understanding of how a location is regarded and rated by industry peers in today's era of social networks, user-generated content and seemingly endless data streams. A notable disconnect or contrast between peer commentary and a location's marketing efforts will only fuel suspicion among investors that the location's credentials don't match the hype and are not necessarily all they're made out to be.

- **Know your competitors – and know them all** – Your competitors may be neighbouring cities, regions and countries, but they may also be on the other the side of the world. Places should have an in-depth and up-to-date understanding of strengths, weaknesses, opportunities and threats (SWOT) in relation to each of these competitors.

- **Be clear about your objectives** – Public sector leaders are often pressured by various local interest groups into claiming that their location can be all things to everyone, but when public resources are stretched, spending comes under ever closer scrutiny and it is therefore essential to be clear where your place's competitive strengths lie, and ensure these strengths are aligned with your goals and objectives and subsequently integrated into marketing campaigns that will deliver the greatest return on investment.

- **Reputations are built from both rational and emotional elements** – A place branding campaign needs to find a rational and an emotional balance which works with its audience. While investment decisions ultimately need to be justified to a company's stakeholders through rational arguments, emotional elements can nevertheless move and capture the imagination of us all (including the CEOs of multinational corporations), so these also have a part to play in investment decisions, not to mention decisions involving the relocation of a company's top talent and their families.

- **Strength through collaboration** – Efforts should be made to co-ordinate messaging from the place's various public bodies. Domestic or local communities and the diaspora should be engaged, as should a place's key companies. Think of the important contribution strong corporate brands make to a place's image, whether national or local: for example, think of the strong association between Sony and Japan, or Armani and Italy. At the more regional or local level, think of the strong association between Apple and California, or BMW and Munich.

- **World-class events can act as brand-building catalysts** – Hosting a world-class event like the Olympics or an international summit puts a spotlight on the country or city, and this should be leveraged to best effect as it can help boost FDI promotion campaigns – we saw a prime example of this in the run up to and during London 2012, when UK Trade & Investment hosted a Global Investment Summit on the eve of the opening ceremony, as well as a host of other investment-related events in tandem with the Olympics. Having a major presence at key international events such as the World Economic Forum in Davos can also ensure international exposure for your place brand.

- **Architecture as a potent brand image** – The physical environment is an important part of a place's brand, and can signal a powerful emotional image. Landmark buildings and skylines should therefore be leveraged as part of a place's marketing and communications campaign.

PLACE BRANDING IN ACTION: CASE STUDIES

Now let us examine a few examples of places that have built and sustained successful brands, as well as ones which have been less successful, in order to draw some lessons from their experiences. Given the ever-increasing importance of cities in the global FDI landscape, we'll start by examining a couple of city brands, before looking at a variety of country brands.

Copenhagen

Copenhagen's relatively new brand, 'OPEN Copenhagen', is a prime example of an initiative that has embraced the concept of brand openness in place of brand ownership. The brand's open source approach enables visitors to access a dedicated website to tailor the badge and strapline to suit their individual needs and wishes via an online tool. The default tagline – 'Open for You' – reinforces the image of a city which puts its audience first.

Figure 2.1   Open city, open brand
Source: www.opencopenhagen.com.

The brand's open source feature has been put to great effect time and again as Copenhagen has played host to international events: in 2009, when the city hosted the UN Climate Change Conference, the COP15 logo was integrated in the badge, while the strapline was tailored to read: 'Open for Change'. Like all good brands, however, Copenhagen's brand architecture is only a reflection of the city's attributes and values, which are demonstrated through its governance, businesses and people.

Copenhagen's accolades are as numerous as they are impressive: the city ranked fifth both for the top northern European cities and for the business-friendliness of major European cities in *fDi Magazine*'s 'European Cities and Regions of the Future 2010–2011'. Copenhagen Capacity, the city's investment promotion agency, was recently named the World's Best Regional IPA by the World Bank, 'Europe's Best Strategy for Capital City Promotion' by the *Financial Times*, while *Forbes* magazine named Denmark the 'World's Best Country for Doing Business' three years in a row (2008–2010). Quality of life is also an important attribute for attracting leading and increasingly discerning talent, and again Copenhagen scores highly in this area – the British magazine *Monocle* ranked Copenhagen the world's third 'Most liveable City' in 2011.

Singapore

Singapore is multi-island microstate which is highly dependent on trade. As such, its primary objective when it comes to place branding has long been to leverage the state's image to boost GDP.

Singapore has often been referenced as the benchmark in city state branding: Dubai, a success story and arguably a role model in its own right, is reported to have looked to Singapore as it underwent its transformation from remote desert emirate to world-leading metropolis and regional hub. Just like Copenhagen, Singapore's brand identity puts its audience first with the use of the tagline 'YourSingapore', and displays the city's commitment to openness – a value and attribute which has long been one of the keystones of Singapore's success as an international business hub.

The global financial crisis had a major impact on FDI inflows to Singapore, yet with the recovery under way, Singapore remains at the forefront of the minds of investors looking at the lucrative Asia-Pacific market. *fDi Magazine* named Singapore as the number one 'Asian City of the Future' in its 2011–12 rankings. Singapore has also claimed the top spot in both the 2010 and 2011 editions of the World Bank's Ease of Doing Business Index.

Pittsburgh

Pittsburgh is a leading example of a city which has undergone a brand transformation in the past few years. In an effort to counter and ultimately overcome Pittsburgh's negative historical image as an old industrial hub in decline, the city re-launched its brand in 2007 with the slogan: 'Pittsburgh. Imagine what you can do here.' This formed part of the Pittsburgh Regional Alliance's efforts to attract talent to the area by promoting the city as a centre of innovation. Pittsburgh is a prime example of a city that has leveraged an international event to promote its brand: since the city hosted the G20 summit in 2009, the Regional Alliance has been responsible for promoting the benefits of conducting business in south-western Pennsylvania to companies worldwide. Pittsburgh was subsequently named as the number one 'Large American City of the Future' by fDi Intelligence in 2011.

*   *   *

Now let's look at some examples of nation brands.

Nigeria

Nigeria's efforts at nation branding in recent years appear to have overlooked many of the truths and golden rules referenced in the previous section. Can Nigeria's recent branding efforts, including Brand Nigeria's tagline 'Good People, Great Nation', be considered to truly reflect the country's realities? Many – both within and outside the country – argue that they don't. Charles O'Tudor, a brand management expert from Lagos, claimed in a recent article that Nigeria's recent rebranding methodology 'has thrown up a myriad of inquiries about our nation's core essence'.[1] O'Tudor rhetorically questioned how Nigeria could 'hope to sweep the decay of several decades under a beautiful carpet of logos and catchphrases? What happens when another Minister comes and jettisons the current rebranding project for a new one?'[2]

Tudor's first question serves to emphasise the importance of grounding reputation-building in reality, while his second question suggests the need for a body which can assume guardianship of the nation's brand and oversee the strategic implementation of a vision that will hopefully last longer than a minister's term in office. While it's true that new leaderships bring new visions (or at least new perspectives on existing visions), a nation's brand, and therefore reputation, cannot realistically be built, let alone sustained, if changes in leadership every few years demand that the nation's brand take a new course and identity. Countries like South Africa have addressed the need for brand continuity with some success, and we will examine this case later.

When it comes to prioritising objectives, Nigeria's efforts can again be brought into question. For example, was it an effective use of resources to channel extensive sums of money and time into developing a national tourism campaign when the country not only has very little in the way of tourism attractions and attributes, but a host of other highly serious problems to address, like regular electricity blackouts, the conflict in the Niger Delta and high levels of corruption, violence and crime?

Such problems are clearly not only impediments to tourism; they're also of major concern to current and would-be foreign investors, as well as Nigerians themselves, of course. We will explore Nigeria's citizens and

---

1   'Rebranding Nigeria', Charles O'Tudor, http://nation-branding.info/2009/03/04/re-branding-nigeria/, 4 March 2009 (accessed 9 July 2012).

2   Ibid.

diaspora more fully in a moment, as they represent two core groups that can help shape Nigeria's reputation for the better. Coming back to the international investment community, recent research indicates that Nigeria's problems have had an adverse effect on the country's reputation among key international stakeholders.

A study on sovereign brands jointly conducted in 2010 by Hill & Knowlton and Penn Schoen Berland surveyed a demographic group known by research firms as 'broad elites'[3] in various countries and assessed their perceptions of 19 sovereign wealth funds (SWFs) and their countries of origin.

When the respondents were asked whether they approved of Nigeria's SWF investing in their country, only 30 per cent did approve, making Nigeria the least-favoured of all SWF investor countries that were surveyed. Respondents were then asked whether or not they felt a list of attributes applied to each SWF country. In the case of Nigeria, its 'strongest' perceived attribute was that it has strong economic potential, with 19 per cent of all respondents seeing this attribute in the country. When it came to political stability and being seen as a trusted member of the global community, only 9 per cent of all respondents said that these attributes applied to Nigeria.

Yet for all these challenges and negative perceptions, Nigeria does have positive stories to tell. Branding experts the world over agree that a brand needs to have internal buy-in if it is to be promoted successfully to external audiences. In an age of social media, this has never been truer – for products, companies and places alike. In the case of Nigeria, the country's diaspora are returning in their droves – according to some reports, more than 10,000 expatriates returned during 2009–2010.[4] This 'brain gain' is precisely what countries like Nigeria need. This return of entrepreneurial talent – largely of Western-educated graduates who have walked away from well-paid jobs and promising careers abroad – is a sure sign of people's optimism about their country's prospects and the massive opportunities it offers them. The challenge will now be to ensure that this elite-driven entrepreneurship and innovation becomes a catalyst for broader investment in Nigeria's education, research and innovation, so that the country becomes a place not only of returning talent, but home-grown talent as well. Only then will 'Brand Nigeria' be able to encapsulate the positive connotations its leaders seek to showcase to the world.

---

3   The socioeconomic research group 'broad elites' is commonly used by market research firms to represent a nation's decision-makers. Broad elites are defined as influential members of society who are university-educated, earning in excess of £50,000 or the local market equivalent, and with an active interest in national and international affairs in the both politics and business.

4   'How Africa is Becoming the New Asia', Jerry Guo, *Newsweek*, 1 March 2010, p. 45.

Egypt

On the other side of the African continent, Egypt – a similar-sized country to Nigeria, both economically and geographically – has a very different brand story to tell. Firstly, to examine the brand of a nation which since early 2011 has been in the throes of a dramatic and at times revolutionary upheaval is a daunting and complex task, yet one we shouldn't shy away from. At the time of writing, Egypt's brand destiny still very much hung in the balance following the country's presidential election in June 2012 and the subsequent prospect of an established, sustainable system of democracy.

Yet in spite of the revolution, some longer-term, positive strands still hold true. Beyond the revolutionary strand, Egypt's brand story over the past decade or so has essentially been one of evolution and diversification. When your country was host to one of the greatest and best-known ancient civilisations in history, it's hard to imagine how this could not be the ultimate brand attribute. So Egypt will always be the land of pyramids and pharaohs. But modern-day Egypt – with its booming population of more than 75 million where the median age is just 24 – is not content to be a museum and a playground for divers and sun-seeking tourists.

The country has a highly developed ICT industry and talent base, so the Egyptian Government established the Information Technology Industry Development Agency (ITIDA) to develop the country's position as a world-leading outsourcing destination by attracting FDI to the country's industry as well as maximising exports of ICT services and applications. The global ICT services marketplace is crowded, with India and China as major industry players. An in-depth analysis of Egypt's investment climate and IT business attributes was therefore needed to advise the development of a brand platform that would differentiate the country's ICT and outsourcing industries. Talent lay at the heart of this brand platform – talent drawn from Egypt's abundant pool of highly skilled and multilingual graduates. This core attribute was the keystone for the subsequent brand-building campaign which covered a broad range of activities, from a comprehensive communications programme to brand architecture development. Within eight months of launching the campaign, Egypt entered the Gartner top 30 outsourcing destinations and won 'Outsourcing Destination of the Year'.

More recently, the uncertainty and violence has clearly had a negative impact on FDI confidence in Egypt, where inflows fell from US$6.4 billion in 2010 to just US$500 million in 2011.[5] Time will tell whether Egypt's FDI prospects

---

5   *Investment Trends Monitor* no. 8.

will improve; in late 2011, Czech Pegas, one of Europe's leading producers of synthetic textiles, announced it would be building a factory in the country; the so-called 'Twitter Revolution' has helped raise global perceptions of Egypt as a tech-savvy country, and there's every possibility that 'first-mover' foreign investors could reap significant rewards and create a virtuous circle where increased FDI could unlock domestic potential. So far, the country's FDI green shoots have been modest and the investment 'renaissance' Egypt is hoping for has yet to come about; what is clear, however, is that the country has many promising brand attributes to help turn this ambition into a reality.

Switzerland

Where Egypt's brand development has focused on dispelling stereotypes and showcasing a fresh, alternative side to the country, Switzerland's has on the contrary been a question of cementing and leveraging its long-standing brand attributes. For centuries, Switzerland has been a bastion of quality, luxury and precision. This latter attribute is probably still best manifested through the country's watchmaking industry. In more recent times, Switzerland's considerable attributes in science, technology and healthcare have showcased Switzerland not only as a country of precision, but of innovation, too. For example, Switzerland's position at the forefront of nuclear science is evident through the country's hosting of the European Organization for Nuclear Research (CERN), a pan-European scientific venture with 20 member states which in turn is one of numerous examples of another key Swiss brand attribute: internationalism. As the home of many of the United Nations' organisations and agencies, Geneva truly is a world city which has contributed considerably to Switzerland's brand image as an open country at one of Europe's most important geographical, linguistic and cultural crossroads, and an international hub over the past fifty years. More business-focused attributes, such as the country's taxation regimes, have also been key to attracting numerous non-European multinationals seeking to establish their European or EMEA[6] headquarters.

35

Switzerland's investment attributes are showcased well beyond its borders, however. For example, the government's initiative in promoting its science and technology credentials abroad through a global network of outposts managed by the State Secretariat for Education and Research has gone a great way to fostering scientific and technological innovation, bilateral co-operation as well as FDI. These and other public–private initiatives are co-ordinated by Presence Switzerland – the state-run organisation dedicated to defining, protecting and promoting the country's brand, built around three

---

6   Europe, Middle East and Africa.

key aspects: 'core messages', 'tonality' and 'appearance'. The core messages used to promote Switzerland internationally are: 'secure future' and 'self-determination', and each is equipped with a list of proof points and stories which underpin these messages.

Figure 2.2   A visual representation of Brand Switzerland, as defined by the Federal Department of Foreign Affairs

Source: Graphic Courtesy of the Federal Department of Foreign Affairs' 'Image Switzerland' website: www.image-schweiz.ch.

Switzerland's methodical and thorough approach to nation branding and its innovative investment promotion efforts appear to have paid major dividends over recent years; UNCTAD ranked Switzerland as the world's sixth largest outward investor in 2010, with FDI outflows of US$58 billion, while the Anholt-GfK Roper Nation Brands Index ranked Switzerland in eighth place in both 2009 and 2010. Meanwhile, the country has taken the number one spot in the World Economic Forum's Global Competitiveness Index since 2009.[7]

---

7   *Global Competitiveness Report 2011–2012*, World Economic Forum, September 2011, p. 349.

All of these rankings arguably portray a country which punches well above its weight when it comes to investment prospects and brand equity.

South Africa

Returning now to Africa, the continent's other economic powerhouse, South Africa, has had mixed success when it comes to its national brand and reputation. The post-apartheid era and the country's iconic leaders in the shape of Nelson Mandela and Archbishop Desmond Tutu have certainly projected a powerful cultural and political image of South Africa to the world. More recently, the 2010 FIFA World Cup truly showcased South Africa as a country that can skilfully host one of the world's greatest events and reinvigorated a sense of national pride.

Yet the World Cup has certainly not been a silver bullet for a host of problems that continue to beset South Africa and its international reputation. An analysis of international media coverage of South Africa conducted by research firm Commetric in June–September 2010 revealed that the country's association with apartheid was the most-covered topic during that period (which included the World Cup).[8] According to the same analysis, other topics that continue to generate significant coverage in international media include reports of corruption among leading figures, high levels of crime and the country's strikes. This serves as a reminder of how global events don't only put their hosts in the spotlight, but under the microscope too, and issues such as the ones covered by the media in the run-up to and during the World Cup are clearly of great concern to any potential foreign investor.

In addition to addressing these important issues, one of South Africa's major challenges is now to build on the confidence, pride and enthusiasm injected into the country by the 2010 World Cup. A public body dedicated to marketing Brand South Africa to the world – the International Marketing Council – is spearheading this renewed effort, and much like the case of Presence Switzerland, it serves as a good example of a national organisation dedicated to ensuring that the country's messaging is as co-ordinated and as unified as possible.

---

8   Commetric analysed 279 articles between 10 June 2010 and 23 September 2010. The coverage source was top global English-language media, and 36 articles talked about South Africa's association with apartheid.

THE CHALLENGE OF CONTINENTAL BRANDING: THE CASE OF AFRICA

We have looked at three examples of nation brands in Africa – Nigeria, Egypt and South Africa – and each has its own very particular history and traits. What perspectives, therefore, are there for continental brands? Is it possible – or worthwhile – to build a brand for a continent like Africa?

Before asking ourselves whether a brand for Africa can be built, we should take a step back and ask ourselves two fundamental questions: firstly, do brands need to be built in order to exist, and secondly, does Africa already have a brand? If we come back to our original premise that reputations form the basis of all brands, then clearly brands do not necessarily need to be built in order to exist. Brands the world over exist in spite of (or in some cases in the absence of) a concerted brand-building effort, and nowhere is this truer than with place brands.

In the case of Africa, the unfortunate reality is that a very negative continental image – fuelled by endless stories of piracy, corruption, pestilence, famine and war – continues to be portrayed to the world. These stories form the basis of a very one-dimensional reputation that can often sideline (or worse still, omit) more positive stories coming out of Africa. That our news is dominated by such negative stories should not come as a surprise, however – the revelation and exposure of corruption, injustice and tragedy has long been a greater priority for journalists than reporting on positive stories, and there's no reason why this principle would change. Yet triumph in the face of adversity is another popular basis for news, as it captures people's hearts and minds. The good news is that such stories are forming the backbone of an increasing number of African news items. These stories – grounded in reality with compelling evidence – which, if told in sufficient quantity, will help to dispel myths and deeply held beliefs, ultimately shaping Africa's reputation for the better. To attempt to rebrand Africa through a centralised, co-ordinated approach, however, would be like trying to turn around an oil tanker – long, slow and very expensive. To brand a corporation of several thousand people or a country of several million is one matter; to attempt to brand a continent of 1 billion people from 53 nations that collectively speak over 1,000 languages is quite another, and nigh on impossible. And yet within Africa, regional groupings such as the East African Community (which, as was mentioned in Chapter 1, could very possibly integrate into a full political union within the next decade) are sure signs that shared international values and visions (two core building blocks of brands) can be applied to a successful entity which transcends borders and can be considered truly African (even if not pan-African).

Lessons for Africa in continental brand development can also be drawn from Asia, which as late as the 1980s was still broadly seen as a continent of great poverty and underdevelopment. Today, in contrast, Asia has become synonymous with growth, dynamism and drive – from the continent's headline-grabbing powerhouses India and China to smaller yet equally innovative and promising economies like South Korea, Vietnam and the Philippines. Strong corporate brands from Asia have also fuelled the continent's reputation as a place of growth and prosperity. In the case of China, investors across the world focus on home-grown brands that have become industry players of global proportions through successfully dominating the huge domestic market (think of Baidu or China Mobile). Meanwhile, India has proven that its entrepreneurial elite can compete successfully with the world's greatest corporations (TATA now owns former British brand icons Jaguar, Land Rover and even Tetley Tea!). Add to these more long-standing iconic Asian corporate brands such as Sony, Toyota and Samsung and a clear picture of the continent's corporate strengths and confidence emerges. When it comes to Africa, however, no such iconic corporate brands immediately spring to mind at present, yet it is the continent's entrepreneurial dynamism and emerging corporate icons which will dispel the long-held myth that the continent is a charity case, and instead portray a rising Africa full of promise and hope.

Just as strong corporate brands can help build strong place brands (and vice versa), weak or negative place brands and brand associations can have a significant bearing on corporations and other organisations from that country looking to invest internationally – broadly referred to in marketing circles as the 'country of origin' effect.

On one level, an investor's efforts to successfully enter a foreign marketplace might be hampered by a weak or even non-existent association between their country of origin and the industry in question. For example, a Hungarian brand of trainers might be highly successful in its domestic market, where its retro style and brand legacy is popular among consumers. Yet if that company seeks to enter the next phase of its growth by planning an expansion into neighbouring countries where the company's brand legacy has no cultural significance or emotional pull, and where Hungary has no broader international reputation in clothing and fashion, then its export and foreign investment plans are likely to be hampered or quite simply brought to a standstill, with all the potentially major commercial implications this limitation might entail for the company and its future prospects in a competitive industry where trends and fads are constantly evolving.

Weak or non-existent brand associations are certainly an impediment to FDI, yet *negative* brand associations are far more challenging and difficult to overcome. Take, for example, the case of Dubai Ports World's attempted acquisition of six port terminals in the United States from P&O back in late 2005, which was met with considerable opposition and hostility from many of the USA's leading political figures, primarily on the grounds that the acquisition of such strategically important national assets would compromise national security. That the investor was from the Middle East only served to fuel opposition among many; the fact that the investor was more specifically from Dubai in the UAE – a long-standing US ally (and a host to the US Navy in the Persian Gulf no less) – was not enough to assuage the critics. The four months of debate which ensued (and which coincided with the run-up to the 2006 US mid-term elections) divided the country's political leaders. Nevertheless, the opponents won when Dubai Ports World was pressured into selling the operations it had acquired from P&O to American International Group.

This debacle was a stark wake-up call for Dubai and how it perceived its standing in the world. If Dubai was to become an admired metropolis and a trusted commercial hub, a major international branding effort would be required – one which would showcase Dubai – and crucially, its numerous state-run entities and enterprises – to the rest of the world. Five years on, and many cities elsewhere in the Gulf and around the world are now seeking to emulate Dubai's achievements, which – as we saw in Chapter 1 – have been impressive in terms of investor confidence and activity.

However, the Dubai Ports World fiasco was far from being an isolated case. Governments and authorities the world over continue to employ a myriad of justifications to pursue protectionist policies against foreign investors and FDI projects. Some of these measures are clearly grounded in rational commercial and socioeconomic justifications, while others often seem to be based on emotionally driven and populist campaigns to suit a certain political agenda. These measures are not always surprising, and nor – in certain cases – are they necessarily wrong. We have seen that a place's brand can be a great asset to FDI agendas – whether outward or inward – yet the vast majority of FDI projects cannot merely rely on and leverage their country of origin's good name and brand. It's an important advantage and a great starting point, but individual foreign investors will face specific sets of challenges – and the communications strategy they employ with relevant stakeholders will often make the difference between a successful and a failed investment, as Chapter 3 explores.

Dubai Ports World: Country-of-origin reputation matters. When the proposed Dubai Ports World acquisition of six port terminals in the USA was halted by the US authorities in 2006, Dubai recognised that a global programme of engagement and communication would be needed to dispel myths and concerns and to counter future potential protectionist measures

Source: Dubai Ports World.

3 Protectionism and Neo-imperialism

Britishers came to India for trade but then ruled us for 250 years. You want to make us slaves once again?

Anna Hazare, activist, November 2011 (speaking in response to proposed FDI in India's multi-brand retail sector).

Protectionist stances – as we saw with the case of Dubai Ports World in Chapter 2 – represent a major challenge for today's foreign investors, even in a world where FDI is in shorter supply than it once was and where there is increasing demand. When the G20 met in Canada in June 2010, the leaders pledged to combat and resist protectionism by not imposing new trade and investment barriers or raising existing ones. However, a research report on 'G20 Protection in the Wake of the Great Recession' produced later that month by the Washington, DC-based Peterson Institute for International Economics (PIIE) stated that G20 countries had 'hundreds of protectionist measures "in the pipeline", ready for implementation',[1] and concluded that the global economy would be confronted with a major protectionist problem even if only half of those measures were implemented.

The sources of protectionist stances and consequent measures tend to be both complex and numerous, incorporating political, economic and social considerations. Governments and other elected authorities face pressures from an array of national and local stakeholders to protect their strategic assets, industries and flagship companies from the threat of foreign competition or acquisition. In the current climate of economic turbulence and uncertainty, governments are increasingly finding themselves conflicted between the need to attract constructive and sparser FDI which will aid economic development,

---

1 *G-20 Protection in the Wake of the Great Recession,* International Chamber of Commerce, prepared by the Peterson Institute for International Economics, 28 June 2010.

foster innovation, transfer technology and create jobs, and pressures to resist FDI which merely seeks to snap up a country's assets 'on the cheap' without benefiting the wider population (and in some cases has a negative impact on them), such as redundancies resulting from cross-border M&A activities.

PROTECTIONISM IN THE WEST

The United States provides a clear illustration of these conflicting pressures. On the one hand, the US administration demonstrated its openness and commitment towards welcoming FDI with the establishment of an Invest in America office within the Department of Commerce in 2007 which, as we saw in Chapter 1, has since been renamed SelectUSA and is set to have a much greater mandate and budget from 2013 onwards.[2] This and a host of other factors, such as the country's all-powerful brand, help to explain why the USA continues to attract more FDI than any other country worldwide and is the leading developed country when it comes to investor confidence.[3] At the same time, however, the country's post-9/11 environment has unsurprisingly given rise to heightened concerns and a sense of priority around national security – a concept which covers not only military security, but also what the Department for Homeland Security refers to as 'critical infrastructure' – a grouping whose definition can potentially cover a vast range of industries and sectors. It is defined as: 'systems and assets ... so vital to the United States that the incapacity and destruction of such systems and assets would have a debilitating impact on security, national economic security, national public health or safety, or any combination of those matters'. The Dubai Ports World case is a prime example of this principle in action.

Across the Atlantic, European countries have also been swift to introduce measures that can arguably be deemed protectionist. As the global economic crisis exploded in late 2008, France's President Nicolas Sarkozy announced the creation of a Strategic Investment Fund (SIF) – the country's own Sovereign Wealth Fund (SWF) – endowed with €20 billion. France's fund differed from most other SWFs in one crucial way, however: while SWFs typically invest abroad, the SIF was established to invest solely in France's domestic market by supporting the development of the country's innovative small and medium-sized enterprises (SMEs), and to stabilise major French companies considered to be of strategic importance to the nation's economy. While the SIF is a

---

2   'President Obama Issues Call to Action to Invest in America at White House "Insourcing American Jobs" Forum', White House press release, http://www.whitehouse.gov/the-press-office/2012/01/11/president-obama-issues-call-action-invest-america-white-house-insourcing?goback=%2Egmp_4046478%2Egde_4046478_member_89358601, 11 January 2012 (accessed 9 July 2012).

3   *Cautious Investors Feed a Tentative Recovery.*

strong indicator of France's current penchant for state intervention, and even state capitalism, the SIF has nevertheless proven through collaboration with foreign SWFs such as the UAE's Mubadala[4] that it is far from being a closed, introverted body, and on the contrary, is fully open to international co-operation and partnerships that can help to advance France's investment interests. On the other hand, the SIF's privileged access to state intelligence inevitably distinguishes it from foreign investor competition, and thus gives weight to the argument that the fund is somewhat protectionist.

For all the trade and investment that criss-crosses the Atlantic in both directions between the world's two largest economies every year, protectionism nevertheless remains a thorn in the side of transatlantic relations, leading in many cases to major trade disputes. One of the most important and bitter of these has been the six-year stand-off between the EU and the USA on their respective aviation industries. Aviation has long been an industry charged with potent national symbolism. Airlines were for a long time (and in some cases still are) the nation's key flag bearers. For some, they even came to represent their countries in far-off, remote corners of the world. The recent troubles facing these traditional airlines – from soaring fuel prices to the rapid rise of low-budget airlines – has prompted countries like Italy and the Czech Republic to prop up their ailing national airlines with state funding. It is the airline manufacturing industry, however, that has been the subject of the most intense transatlantic trade dispute in recent years – and the largest ever brought before the World Trade Organisation (WTO). Europe's Airbus consortium and the USA's Boeing – which have significant investments and are major employers in the US and Europe respectively – have been at loggerheads over alleged illegal state aid on both sides, and in the past couple of years the WTO has issued rulings that both companies have benefited from illegal government aid, distorting market competition. In June 2010, the WTO ruled that Airbus's A380 Superjumbo had received illegal export subsidies from the UK, Spain and Germany,[5] while in January 2011, it was Boeing's turn to come into the firing line when the WTO ruled that the US giant had also benefited from illegal subsidies.[6] These rulings, combined with the rise of aggressive competition from China and Brazil's aerospace

---

4   Collaboration between the SIF and Mubadala took the form of a Memorandum of Understanding. More information available at: http://www.fonds-fsi.fr/fr-fr/les-partenaires/le-fonds-mubadala.html (accessed 9 July 2012).

5   'Subsidies for Airbus Illegal, Says WTO', Joshua Chaffin, FT.com, http://www.ft.com/cms/s/0/624f7e0c-845e-11df-9cbb-00144feabdc0.html#axzz1Dr7OIz00, 30 June 2010 (accessed 9 July 2010).

6   'WTO Rules Boeing Had Illegal Subsidies', Peggy Hollinger, FT.com, http://www.ft.com/cms/s/0/380c7d6c-2d86-11e0-8f53-00144feab49a.html#axzz1Dr7OIz00, 31 January 2011 (accessed 9 July 2012).

industries, have lent a new sense of urgency to establishing an international set of rules on acceptable forms of state aid and aircraft financing.

PROTECTIONISM IN EMERGING MARKETS

While emerging markets are now increasingly outward investors in Western and other developed markets, many nevertheless continue to adopt protectionist measures when it comes to inward FDI and imports into their markets. According to Global Trade Alert's 2012 report on protectionism, the top three countries identified as having imposed discriminatory measures were Russia, Argentina and India, followed by the UK, Germany, France and China.[7]

In Russia, protectionist measures have been numerous and diverse. One of the first industries to see the introduction of protectionist measures with the onset of the economic crisis at the end of 2008 was agriculture: duties on meat and agriculture equipment imports were hiked in December as the country's farming industry felt the brunt of the crisis. This was closely followed by new, higher duties on foreign car imports in January 2009 as domestic manufacturers' market share was giving way to foreign brands.

In India, legislation limits foreign ownership of domestic businesses in various sectors. A 26 per cent foreign ownership limit in the insurance sector garnered high-profile criticism in early 2011 when the iconic US investor Warren Buffett claimed on a visit to Bangalore that the limit served as a deterrent to investment from his holding company Berkshire Hathaway.[8] The most high-profile and widely reported case of foreign ownership limits in India relates to the retail sector, however. In later 2011, the Indian government proposed relaxing the rules on FDI in the sector by allowing foreign firms 51 per cent ownership in multi-brand retail enterprises and 100 per cent in single-brand ones.[9] The proposals sparked widespread protests from broad sections of society in a country where there are an estimated 5–8 million family-run *kiranas* (or 'mom & pop' grocery stores). These protests forced the government to make a U-turn on its proposed plans for multi-brand retail, and at the time of writing, a roadmap acceptable to India's key stakeholders was still in

---

7   *Débâcle: 11th GTA Report on Protectionism*: http://www.globaltradealert.org/sites/default/files/GTA11_0.pdf (accessed 11 August 2012).

8   'Buffett Says India Insurance Ownership Limit Deters Berkshire Investment', Pooja Thakur and Jay Shankar, Bloomberg, http://www.bloomberg.com/news/2011-03-23/buffett-says-india-insurance-ownership-limit-deters-investment.html, 23 March 2011 (accessed 9 July 2012).

9   'Multi-brand retail' refers to stores such as supermarkets where a variety of brands are on sale, while 'single-brand' applies to stores that sell products under one brand name only.

development. The single-brand retail market has since opened up, however, with the ratification of the government's proposed full ownership proposal in January 2012. This has prompted concern and objections from multi-brand retail multinationals such as Walmart and Tesco which have long been keen to penetrate India's promising fast-moving consumer goods market and who may now be at a disadvantage compared to single-brand competitors such as Marks & Spencer.

UNDERSTANDING PROTECTIONISM

The steps taken to protect Russia's agricultural industry or India's micro-retail sector raise important questions around what constitutes protectionism, and even whether all protectionism is necessarily bad. The word undoubtedly carries negative connotations in a globalised world where open markets and trade are understood, through laws of economics, to supposedly make everyone better off. A government's first duty is to the people who elected it, however, and no government can allow the industry which produces the nation's food or which guarantees the livelihoods of millions of its citizens to collapse.

The automotive sector – like many other industries – is another matter, as the most fundamental elements of a country's existence are arguably not at stake (although plenty of other important interests are, of course). The usual motives behind protectionist measures are pretty unsurprising – they usually form the basis of either populist, politicised or practical agendas and programmes (and often a combination of the three): job protection and creation, bilateral and international trade disputes, governmental and party-political popularity-boosters and so on. Russia is an interesting case within the group of emerging markets in the sense that only a few decades ago, not only was it arguably emerged, it was a global leader in a bi-polar world. More than twenty years have now passed since the fall of the Berlin Wall, and many of Russia's political and business leaders today barely recall what Communism was like (indeed, for an increasing number of them, it's confined to the annals of history). Today's Russian elite have embraced Western capitalism in the firms they work for, the clothes they wear, the cars they drive and the food they eat – all to the great benefit of international investors. Yet to dismiss or overlook the enduring nature of national identities can potentially result in FDI setbacks, barriers and challenges.

A separate book could be written on the influence of national identities and historic international relations on FDI, and Chapter 5 explores this topic to some extent by looking at the influence exerted by diplomacy and geopolitics. Suffice it to make the point here that the country which put the first man into space while its people queued for bread had a leadership with visions of grandeur and pride, and while prioritising rockets over food would clearly be unacceptable in today's Russia, the country's current leadership – and particularly Vladimir Putin, the man who many believe gave Russia back her sense of pride through the country's sharp economic rebound at the turn of the century – see great political benefit in playing the populist card which argues that the assets of a great country like Russia are not to become 'easy pickings' for foreign investors.

Foreign investors always need to understand the historical context within which they operate – or seek to operate. In the case of China – currently the world's largest emerging market host country for FDI – that important historical context goes back to the mid-nineteenth century and the opium wars through which the Chinese suffered what it saw as a series of humiliating defeats by Britain and other Western powers. At the heart of these wars – and the subsequent concessions which were made by the Chinese – was trade. In the case of Hong Kong, it even meant the loss of territory following the Treaty of Nanking in 1842. China's famous 'century of humiliation' had begun. The country which reassumed sovereignty over Hong Kong in 1997, however, could not have been more transformed. As the new millennium approached, it was clear that China was set to become a global power; its century of humiliation was at an end, and a century of great promise lay ahead.

Far from renouncing the principles of international trade which had so repelled imperial China in the nineteenth century, today's China clearly embraces them. Africa in many ways presents the same solutions and opportunities to the Chinese today that China itself presented to a rapidly industrialising Britain in the nineteenth century. The terms of engagement have certainly evolved (the threat of war is no longer an 'incentive' to open one's territory to trade), and China's role in Africa will be examined in more detail later in this chapter. The fact remains, however, that China's enduring prosperity depends upon a world which remains open to its investments and its exports, even while domestic demand and consumption are on the rise.

However, China also pursues protectionist agendas that have significant implications for FDI. Since the onset of the global economic downturn, European and US businesses have been voicing increasing concerns over protectionist Chinese policies aimed at restricting technological FDI in favour of domestic technologies, and thus boosting exports. At a US-China strategic and economic dialogue in May 2010, senior US trade representative Ron Kirk went so far as to assert that resolving these protectionist issues was of greater importance to US interests than the prominent discussions around the undervaluation of the Chinese currency, the yuan. [10]

China also faces outward FDI challenges. Much of the country's international investment is carried out by entities which are either fully or partially owned by the state, arousing suspicion among some international partners that their investments are politically as well as commercially driven. Even in the case of reportedly private Chinese firms, doubts over links to the state have fuelled concerns over the security implications of their investments. Take the case of Huawei as an example: the company's unsuccessful bid to acquire a stake in US firm 3Com in 2008 was partly attributed to decision-makers' concerns around economic and national security implications. Two years later, when Huawei sought to acquire 2Wire and Motorola's wireless equipment unit in 2010, the bid was also rejected by US authorities, once again on grounds of national security, among others. This was in spite of the fact that Huawei's bids for both assets were US$100 million higher than competing offers.[11]

Then there are the sovereign wealth funds. These are broadly seen as a major new force in global economics, and China alone has four of them. By the end of 2011, the world's SWFs were estimated to have collective assets worth around US$4.8 trillion[12] (which is roughly the same size as the nominal GDP of Germany – currently the world's fourth largest economy), yet in spite of their size, surprisingly little is known about them. We've already examined France's answer to the emergence of SWFs – to create its own domestic one. But how are SWFs perceived by key stakeholders elsewhere in the world, and what implications do their stances have for the future investment priorities of these gargantuan sources of capital?

WHO'S AFRAID OF THE BIG BAD SWF?

The front cover of a recently published book on the subject of SWFs and their role in the global economy portrays a small piggy bank whose shadow is that of a much larger and menacing wolf. Eric J. Weiner's *The Shadow Market* voices

10 See, for example, an article in *The Telegraph* on this issue: 'Chinese Protectionism, Not the Yuan, is Our Greatest Concern, Says Top US Negotiator', Peter Foster, http://www.telegraph.co.uk/finance/china-business/7764019/Chinese-protectionism-not-the-yuan-is-our-greatest-concern-says-top-US-negotiator.html, 25 May 2010 (accessed 9 July 2012).

11 'Huawei Said to Lose Out on U.S. Assets Despite Higher Offers', Serena Saitto and Jeffrey McCracken, Bloomberg, http://www.bloomberg.com/news/2010-08-02/huawei-said-to-be-stymied-in-purchase-of-u-s-assets-on-security-concerns.html, 3 August 2010 (accessed 9 July 2012).

12 According to the Sovereign Wealth Fund Institute.

the concerns many other stakeholders in the West have expressed towards this largely unfamiliar – and in some cases elusive – breed of investors.

Hill & Knowlton and Penn Schoen Berland's joint study on sovereign brands published in 2010 revealed a strong correlation between lower degrees of familiarity and lower degrees of favourability when it came to perceptions of SWFs. Of more than 1,000 'broad elites' surveyed in seven countries worldwide, only 57 per cent said that they were familiar or somewhat familiar with SWFs – making sovereign wealth the least-known source of investment. When it came to favourability, SWFs, with a mere 19 per cent of respondent support, fared only marginally better than hedge funds (13 per cent), while better-known sources of investment had higher rates of favourability, although none were highly favoured – unsurprising, given the economic climate in which the survey was set. Interestingly, however, investment banks – while being perceived by respondents along with hedge funds as the joint greatest contributor to market turmoil (65 per cent) – nevertheless had the highest favourability ranking, at 36 per cent; they were also the most familiar source of investment. Meanwhile, SWFs were far less associated with contributing to market turmoil (40 per cent).

Crucially, these low levels of familiarity and favourability translated into a heightened sense of concern about SWF investment in relation to other sources of investment; overall, 52 per cent of respondents said they would be either much more or somewhat more concerned if a SWF were to invest in their country compared to other forms of finance, while in China, a staggering 97 per cent expressed such concerns.

These and other indicators suggest that SWFs are confronted with major reputational challenges, and while it is expected that the economic recovery is spurring a renewed interest in SWFs, much remains to be done in terms of convincing key international stakeholders that these massive sources of investment are reliable and trustworthy, thus providing credible and compelling reasons to counterbalance protectionist measures imposed against them.

It is essential that a SWF understands international perceptions of its *country of origin*: 98 per cent of respondents in the sovereign brands study said that the country of origin's reputation was an important factor in determining how positively or negatively a given SWF was perceived, with 68 per cent considering this to be 'very important'. Of the various country attributes that help shape that country's SWF(s), political and economic stability, a commitment to the rule of law and adherence to international regulatory standards were considered the most important by respondents.

When it comes to SWFs specifically, rather than their countries or origin, the most important attributes for respondents were *transparency* (72 per cent), *accountability* (68 per cent) and *good governance* (65 per cent). In order to demonstrate these attributes, an effectively designed and implemented communications strategy is essential. As with any organisation, if stakeholders in target markets are not aware of the fund, its vision and mission, the values it stands for, its governance and interested parties, what its objectives are and its record of action (in the case of a SWF, details of its investment portfolio to date), then there is no basis for trust or confidence in that organisation. The lack of such openness is in itself grounds for suspicion and mistrust, which can in turn lead to protectionism and hostility. The challenge starts with a SWF's website – that most fundamental of communications tools which, even at the time of writing this book, some SWFs did not have. Other SWFs provide links either to their own websites or those of the ministries to which they belong, only for the links to prove unavailable. In early 2011, one SWF in the Middle East only had a single basic homepage with a title, logo and contact details. Even by August 2012 the site's only addition was a message stating that the site was under construction. At this point in time, the SWF in question – Oman's State General Reserve Fund[13] – was reported to have assets in excess of US$ 8 billion, according to the Sovereign Wealth Fund Institute.[14]

CHALLENGING AND COUNTERING PROTECTIONISM

FDI protectionism is likely to remain a major challenge for the foreseeable future. Even in a post-recessionary world where cash-strapped countries, regions and cities desperately scramble for investment to shore up their economies, boost flagging industries and reduce unemployment, decision-makers are all too aware that certain investments come at a heavy – and in some cases potentially detrimental – political price. The cases examined so far in this chapter lead to some key considerations and measures which should be looked at in order to effectively counter, and in some cases challenge, protectionist measures against FDI:

- **Understand sensitivities** – We have already established that protectionism's roots tend to be multifaceted and complex. *Protection* is a core service any government must strive to ensure for its people; *protecting* the national interest has long been the core duty of governments and their administrations. The simple adding of an '-ism' on the end of this core duty seemingly turns a positive concept into a negative one, but if investors do not seek to

13 http://www.sgrf.gov.om/ (accessed 11 August 2012).
14 http://www.swfinstitute.org/fund-rankings/ (accessed 11 August 2012).

understand the root causes and motivating factors behind particular protectionist measures, they will find it difficult to engage decision-makers in seeking a solution that will either address or detract from their sensitivities.

- **What type of protectionism?** – Investors need to understand whether protectionist measures are directed specifically against them, against the wider industry they're in, or whether the target market adopts protectionist measures against foreign investors more broadly. Protectionism against a planned investment by an individual company suggests the need for a corporate reputation-building and public affairs campaign (and potentially issues and crisis management). Industry-specific protectionist measures offer companies with investment interests the opportunity to form alliances that in some cases offer a greater sense of credibility and legitimacy (much in the same way that EU trade associations are sometimes more effective in Brussels-based public affairs than the advocacy efforts pursued individually by companies). Broader protectionism that hinders FDI regardless of industry presents a greater challenge which tends to be addressed by bilateral or multilateral government relations and diplomacy (to be explored further in Chapter 5).

- **Familiarity drives favourability** – If you're not transparent in your activities, or if you don't engage your multiple audiences, then you cannot expect to build trust in your organisation. Without wishing to offend investment banks, the old adage 'better the devil you know' could not find a better example than the SWF study we looked at earlier which showed them to be better-known and more favoured than SWFs, even though the latter were perceived to have contributed less to the economic turmoil. In an information- and data-hungry world where conversation is a constant, silence and covertness only fuel suspicion.

- **Position FDI as a development tool** – FDI is typically a long-term form of investment, not a means of achieving short-term gains. As such, it has the potential to position and prove itself as a partner for development and mutual benefit, instead of a means of merely snapping up a country's assets which benefits the investor and only a small group of 'elites' in the target market.

- **The need to name and shame** – In some cases, countering protectionism will not suffice, and it needs to be challenged.

At present, there is no international framework which actively names and shames individual countries that abuse the use of FDI protectionism measures under questionable guises of protecting the national interest. Many cases are of course not clear-cut, and there's certainly a case to be made for the limited use of measures and mechanisms that protect legitimate national objectives and interests – but no international FDI body dedicated to reviewing issues and disputes on a case-by-case basis currently exists. Calls have rightly been made for the establishment of an FDI Protectionism Observatory[15] or similar body to monitor, and where necessary 'name and shame', countries, regions and cities that disregard international agreements on trade and investment. In exposing such cases of malpractice, there would be some hope that the prospect of being ostracised by the international investment community would spur the decision-makers concerned into reassessing their approach to inward FDI and the limitations they impose.

53

RED AFRICA: CHINESE NEO-IMPERIALISM OR INEVITABLE SYMBIOSIS?

For all the cases and issues of FDI protectionism we have explored, the symbiotic economic relationship between China and Africa seems very much to be an antidote to protectionism. A combination of factors has contributed to the sheer enormity and depth of economic links and transactions between China and numerous African countries. Fundamentally, each side has a vested interest in the assets or attributes of the other: Africa has the wealth of natural resources China needs to fuel its massive manufacturing-intensive economy, while cash-rich China offers seemingly endless infrastructure investment opportunities to help boost African economies, building new roads, schools and hospitals, developing power generation and IT networks – often with very few strings attached. Seen in this light, suggestions of a neo-imperialistic stance on China's part seem out of place, and China is quick to insist that it does not impose its will on African countries. Yet many of the African nations in which China invests have systems of governance that deter investors from the West (more on this later). Thus China time and again becomes the privileged or preferred supplier to governments emboldened by a sense that when other countries hesitate or attach unwelcome conditions to proposed investments, Beijing will be there to seal the deal. But does this reassurance not come at the cost of overdependence on China? Even if individual

---

15 *FDI Protectionism is On the Rise*, Karl P. Sauvant, The World Bank, Poverty Reduction and Economic Management Network, Policy Research Working Paper 5052, September 2009, p. 20.

investments come with few strings attached, the bigger picture suggests a deepening and ever more 'exclusive' relationship from which Africa could find it increasingly difficult to distance itself.

The notion of neo-imperialism is somewhat exaggerated, however: after all, China is heavily dependent on Africa for its own industrial growth, yet unlike Europe in the nineteenth century, it seeks to engage and trade with its African partners, rather than to coerce them (let alone force them) into collaboration – hence the preference to describe the relationship as symbiotic. Of the numerous African workers employed by Chinese firms, many tend to be on lower wages than their Chinese counterparts, but such is the current reality of macroeconomics, and the situation remains the same wherever foreign investors and employers are from (including the West), although it's worth remembering that FDI typically leads to a wage premium, as referenced in this book's Introduction. If anything, Chinese investment is one of the major driving forces behind the rapid growth in Africa's emerging middle class, which according to 2011 estimates from the African Development Bank already constitutes around a third of the continent's entire population, if not more.[16]

WHERE ANGELS FEAR TO TREAD: THE CAUTIOUSNESS OF THE WEST

None of the above serves to, or is intended to, undermine the legitimate concerns expressed by numerous Western governments, international organisations and NGOs. Stories of corruption and human rights abuses still abound in Africa, and the international community is clearly right to push for and support reform. As former colonisers of Africa, the West – and many European countries in particular – inevitably have a heightened sense of dutiful benevolence towards Africa. From the oppression of imperial regimes to the chaos, poverty, famine, conflict and oppression that dominated the first few decades of post-colonial Africa, Europe's history on the continent has not been a proud one. Aid has arguably been the single greatest – and certainly the most visible – driver of Western involvement in Africa over the past few decades. In business and political circles, there's certainly growing acceptance for the argument that trade and investment will be play a crucial part in enabling the continent to grow and prosper, but while stories of corruption and human rights abuses in certain African countries continue

---

16 *The Middle of the Pyramid: Dynamics of the Middle Class in Africa*, African Development Bank, http://www.afdb.org/fileadmin/uploads/afdb/Documents/Publications/The%20 Middle%20of%20the%20Pyramid_The%20Middle%20of%20the%20Pyramid.pdf, 20 April 2011 (accessed 9 July 2012).

to attract international attention and condemnation, these countries can represent operational and reputational risks of such magnitude for would-be investors that any planned investment becomes simply untenable, no matter how lucrative the potential financial gains might be. In short, when a European multinational investor enters Africa, it's under the watchful eyes of interested parties (not least consumers) back home and also in its new host country, which, depending on the investor's country of origin, may throw up a host of challenges, and even hostilities.

Africa clearly offers up a wealth of opportunities to would-be foreign investors – the continent's macroeconomic indicators provide compelling evidence of this. Opportunities need to be weighed up against potential operational and reputational risks, however. FDI projects are typically long-term engagements – short-term gains are therefore not usually enough to warrant such investments. Careful planning and compelling evidence are needed to convince company shareholders, board members and a host of other private and public sector stakeholders that a foreign investment exercise is viable, worthwhile, sustainable and free from significant risk (I add 'significant' because all business ventures inevitably entail some degree of risk).

Chapter 4 analyses the various considerations preying upon investors' minds as they consider where to invest abroad, and which factors influence their decisions.

Old Street Roundabout, East London: The digital cluster and investment hotspot 'Tech City' in London's East End has become a magnet for innovators, entrepreneurs and investors in the digital media space

Source: UK Trade & Investment.

4 The Investor Perspective

An investment in knowledge always pays the best interest.

Benjamin Franklin

Today's international investor is confronted with a far more volatile and uncertain world than before the global economic downturn. While parts of the global economy are now definitely showing strong signs of recovery and FDI activity is on the rise, flows are still lower than they were in 2007 (even though by 2011 they slightly exceeded the pre-crisis average).[1] Access to finance does not appear to be the principal impediment to investment, however. Recent analysis from UNCTAD cites investor concerns over regulatory uncertainty and operational risk as the main factors behind investor reticence, and with the macroeconomic, social and political unrest that has erupted in various parts of the world in 2011, this is understandable.

The sovereign debt crisis that has besieged much of Europe has left many investors wary and in some cases even nervous about the future prospects not only of those countries bailed out by the EU and the IMF (Greece, Portugal and Ireland), but others now in seemingly choppy waters – notably Spain, Italy and to a lesser extent France and even Germany, traditionally Europe's economic powerhouse. The eurozone crisis has alarmed leaders beyond Europe's borders, too: China, the USA and other major global economies have all been calling for Europe's leaders to take bold and decisive action to avoid contagion and the triggering of another global economic crisis.

---

1   World Investment Report 2012 This point is illustrated in Chapter 1 – see Figure 1.1.

Yet the dim macroeconomic outlook is not the only worry preying on foreign investors' minds. The year 2011 arguably went down in history as a one of global social upheaval. When the Tunisian street vendor Mohammed Bouazizi tragically set himself alight in protest against reported harassment by the authorities, his act was the catalyst which ignited the Tunisian revolution, leading to the resignation of President Ben Ali that in turn sparked the infamous Arab Spring which spread throughout the greater Middle East. Meanwhile, in England – traditionally seen as a bastion of stability, law and order – the shooting of Mark Duggan in August 2011 by police in Tottenham, north London, sparked a series of riots that lay siege to homes and businesses in London and elsewhere throughout the country.

Both tragedies demonstrated the ability of one incident to ignite far greater unrest, whether grounded in ideology and a desire for meaningful change, as in the case of Tunisia and subsequently Egypt, Libya and Syria, or grounded in reckless thuggery and opportunism, as was sadly the case in England. In addition to the numerous homes and small businesses devastated by the England riots, larger businesses and international investors were also hit. Aldi, the German supermarket chain with more than 400 stores in the UK and Ireland, became one of the symbolic corporate victims of the London riots when images of its Tottenham store in flames featured on the front pages of newspapers and websites around the world.

Unanticipated outbursts of violence inevitably have a negative impact on investor confidence in the short to medium term; images, videos and stories of violence and destruction linger in people's minds – including those of investors who have businesses to run, employees to look after and assets to insure. The long-term nature of FDI, however, means that investors, while cautious, will also tend to take a holistic and forward-thinking view of a location's attributes and risks. The reality is that no world city is immune from spates of violence. Paris and other French cities were hit by a similar outburst of riots in November 2005, yet in 2006 France remained a top global location for FDI, coming in third place globally for inflows that year.

WHAT MATTERS TO INVESTORS?

While enduring peace and stability are crucial for garnering investor confidence, a host of other factors and drivers are prime factors when companies are considering whether to invest internationally, and if so, where to locate a given project.

The Talent Imperative

As industries and streams of business become ever more sophisticated and specialised, access to skilled, specialist talent has never been more important. For foreign investors, the success of their activities in foreign markets will depend greatly on being able not only to employ or procure the services of local skilled workers, but in many cases (and for emerging markets in particular) also being able to ensure that top talent in home or existing markets are willing to relocate to ensure successful market entry and crucial knowledge and skills transfer to local employees. On the upside for investors, skilled workers are increasingly mobile and internationally minded, recognising the enhanced career development opportunities a posting abroad can bring – whether short- or long-term. This mobility of top talent inevitably poses challenges for certain locations, however, both in terms of talent attraction and retention. For example, a city or region which is reputed for its universities and higher education institutions yet is otherwise economically depressed is faced with the inevitable challenge of a brain drain. For this reason, many universities increasingly seek to form closer ties with business and industry to form clusters and centres of excellence that bridge the gap between academia, R&D and business. East Anglia in the UK is a prime example of a region that has leveraged its world-renowned 'talent asset' – Cambridge University – to attract world-leading multinationals to the region, forming industrial clusters in sectors such as biotechnology and medical devices, aerospace, renewable energy and IT services. The latter cluster includes world-leading technology firms such as Microsoft, Toshiba, 3Com, Sony and Qualcomm, and has led many to refer to the region as 'Silicon Fen'.

fDi Markets data for 2011 reveal that when it comes to selecting a foreign location for R&D investment, access to skills is typically the most important deciding factor. China is the exception to this rule, where markets are the number one determinant, as Figure 4.1 demonstrates. This is perhaps somewhat unsurprising given China's massive economic potential, yet in Asia's other economic powerhouse, India, skills far outweigh markets in terms of importance. The same is true of more developed economies like the USA, Singapore and the UK. It is therefore crucial that economic development organisations focus on collaborating with universities and other higher education institutions to ensure that their location's talent attributes make a compelling value proposition to would-be investors, and while it would be a step too far to claim that higher education is merely a conduit for the needs of business, if there are major disconnects between these needs and the talent offer, then this should be addressed for the well-being and future prosperity of that economy.

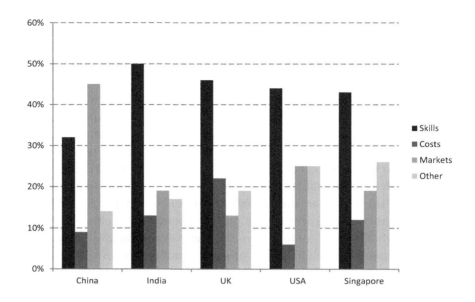

Figure 4.1   Drivers of R&D investments by location
Source: fDi Markets, 2011 www.fDiMarkets.com.

Market Access and Potential

Access to new markets and customers as a means of supporting business growth is frequently cited as the main driver behind FDI decisions, and is often given more importance than cost-saving considerations. In A.T. Kearney's 2010 Investor Confidence Index, 63 per cent of respondents rated 'access to new markets' as the most important driver of investment decisions. This compares with 24 per cent who saw cutting costs as a main driver, while financial subsidies and tax exemptions were considered even less important as drivers (only 10 per cent and 9 per cent respectively). Once it has been established that the market potential of a nation or a region warrants investment, a rigorous selection process typically follows and will cover an extensive list of considerations.

Ease of market access and doing business will be at or near the top of the list of investors' considerations. How long will it take to set up a business or a subsidiary in a given location? What administrative and legal requirements, procedures and costs will be incurred? What is the current corporate tax rate and regime? How is this predicted to evolve in the months and years to come, and how does this compare with other locations in the region? What tax incentives are offered? How does the operational landscape for foreign companies compare with domestic ones, and where applicable, how does this position an investor in relation to its local competitors?

Location, Location, Location

Geography and infrastructure also play an important role in determining a location's suitability as a springboard for wider market access, particularly in the case of regional headquarters and manufacturing hubs. Many of the world's most successful FDI hotspots are cities that are easily accessible from all parts of their wider region and have impressive infrastructure amenities to match. For example, Dubai sits comfortably between the prosperous economies of the Persian Gulf to the west and the Indian subcontinent to the east, while both Western Europe and East Asia are less than a seven-hour flight away. These geographic advantages are capitalised upon by a world-class airport, an airline (Emirates) with a route network that is unrivalled anywhere else in the region, as well as a world-class set of maritime ports.

Similarly, Hong Kong, whose Chep Lak Kok airport was recently voted the best airport in the world by international travellers, sits on the tip of one of the world's most densely populated and rapidly industrialising regions, the Pearl River delta region. Roughly similar in geographical size to Northern Ireland, the Pearl River delta has a population of around 120 million, according to recent UN estimates – if it were a country, it would be the world's eleventh most populated. It is also geographically nestled in between China's political and economic powerhouses to the north (Beijing and Shanghai), the dynamic emerging economies of the Philippines, Indonesia, Malaysia and Vietnam to the south and east, and India to the west.

The FDI results speak for themselves: Hong Kong, with US$83 billion of inflows, was the third largest recipient of FDI globally in 2011, up from US$71 billion in 2010, US$52 billion in 2009 and second only to mainland China in the Asia-Pacific region.[2] Meanwhile, foreign investors recently named Dubai their preferred location in the Middle East, citing ease of doing business, best-in-class infrastructure and advanced logistics facilities as some of the emirate's key investment attributes.[3]

Birds of a Feather Flock Together

The example of Cambridge and East Anglia mentioned earlier demonstrates the benefits brought to a regional economy by clusters and centres of excellence. A world-leading university or higher education institution and the talent it 'incubates' is not necessarily the only draw for would-be investors, however.

---

2   Ibid.
3   Investing in a Rebound, p. 11.

In 2010, British Prime Minister David Cameron launched Tech City UK, an initiative to develop the existing cluster of technology firms in east London into one of the world's leading centres of IT innovation. The existing cluster of innovative technology firms around Old Street (or 'Silicon Roundabout' as it is affectionately known) and Shoreditch already provided the area with a firm base and compelling set of attributes for encouraging new firms to set up shop in Tech City, from small start-ups to established multinationals. The Tech City Investment Organisation (TCIO), a newly established organisation within UK Trade & Investment dedicated to driving investment into the area, works closely with current and potential investors, providing them with tailored advice and intelligence on key topics such as customer bases, suppliers and recruitment, specialist tax advice, as well as corporate real estate options. Since November 2010, the number of companies in the area has more than doubled, and as of August 2011, Tech City was home to more than 500 digital and technology companies, according to Digital Shoreditch's survey of businesses in the area.

Another leading example of successful clustering is Medicon Valley – a joint initiative by Invest in Skåne (Sweden) and Copenhagen Capacity (Denmark) which has led to the creation of one of Europe's leading life science clusters, bringing together 455 companies, 32 hospitals and 10 universities. A broad range of services is offered to potential investors, including: partner and investment opportunity identification, location services, visiting programmes and benchmark analyses.

Aftercare and the Customer-centric Ethos

With the ever-prevalent scramble for investment attraction, it is sometimes easy to forget that investor retention is just as important. While it is true that FDI, unlike some other forms of investment, tends to take a long-term view, economic development agencies should not consider their job done once the investment signing ceremony has taken place. For a start, effective aftercare can help to nurture an initial investment into something greater (for example, corporate expansion) as investor confidence in their new 'hosts' grows through positive experience. Then there's the importance of corporate advocacy: would-be investors do not merely look at where their peers are located when considering an investment project, they will also tend to look very closely at what these peers have to say about their experiences of operating in those locations. This has long been an important factor for economic development organisations to bear in mind as investors congregate and share experiences through industry gatherings and so forth, yet the rapid rise of social media's influence in the business world has made this even more pressing. Referred to in some circles as the 'TripAdvisor effect', investor commentary and dialogue on social networking sites, in sufficient quantity and potency, arguably has the power to help make or break a location's image among potential investors – this is a topic that will be explored in greater detail in Chapter 6.

THE RELATIVE IMPORTANCE OF RANKINGS

We live in an age of rankings and indices that claim to provide easily digestible insights into the relative attractiveness of locations in terms of a vast range of attributes, including global competitiveness, ease of doing business, quality of life, brand equity, innovation and even peace. While it's natural to want to top rankings and beat your competitors, whatever the field may be, what matters is having an understanding both of the relative importance current and potential investors attach to each ranking or index as well as the methodologies used to compile them.

63

Without an in-depth understanding of the rankings that benchmark locations, economic development organisations are, in the case of a positive ranking, at risk of missing out on important messaging, while with a negative ranking, they are in danger of being unable to credibly detract from the findings and reassure investors of their locations' attributes in spite of a bad result which might arguably be founded on questionable methodology or even factors that are less relevant for FDI.

Here is a list of rankings and indices that economic development organisations should not only be aware of, but also understand deeply and monitor closely.

World Bank's Ease of Doing Business Index

The Ease of Doing Business Index ranks 183 economies on the basis of nine factors which indicate the regulatory environment in each economy. These include: starting a business, dealing with construction permits, registering property, getting credit, protecting investors, paying taxes, trading across borders, enforcing contracts and closing a business.[4] The World Bank is broadly regarded as a leading authority on FDI-related matters, and as such its findings will tend to be closely studied by leading investors.

---

4   A detailed overview of the methodology used in compiling the Ease of Doing Business Index is available at: http://www.doingbusiness.org/~/media/FPDKM/Doing%20 Business/Documents/Reforms/DB10Easeofdoingbusinessrankmethod.pdf (accessed 9 July 2012).

World Economic Forum's Global Competitiveness Index

The World Economic Forum's (WEF) Global Competitiveness Index forms part of the WEF's annual report with the same name and has been measuring national competitiveness since 2005. The index looks at 12 'pillars of competitiveness' (institutions, policies and various micro- and macroeconomic factors) that collectively seek to determine a country's overall competitiveness.[5] Given the WEF's strong private sector contingency, this index is also held in high regard by corporate leaders and investors.

A.T. Kearney's FDI Confidence Index

The FDI Confidence Index is a regular global survey of executives conducted by the management consultancy A.T. Kearney, and has been running since 1998. Participants are selected from companies spanning 17 industry sectors in 44 countries, and the data is used to compile an index of the top 20 countries for investor confidence. The index is formed on a calculated average of low, medium and high responses to questions about the probability of direct investment in a given country over the following three years. With a specific focus on FDI as opposed to broader business topics, this index is widely regarded as one the management consultancy world's leading analyses of investor confidence.[6]

Anholt-GfK Roper's Nation Brands Index and City Brands Index

The Nation Brands Index and City Brands Index were developed in 2005 and 2006 respectively by place branding consultant Simon Anholt, and are now produced on an annual basis in partnership with custom research firm GfK Roper. Simon Anholt is broadly regarded as a leading authority on place branding, and has been an adviser to governments worldwide. The Nation Brands Index ranks countries based on the following factors: exports, governance, culture and heritage, people, tourism, investment and immigration. Meanwhile, the City Brands Index looks at what it refers to as: 'presence, place, pre-requisites, people, pulse and potential'.[7] The indices are limited to 50 countries and 50 cities, however, so being featured in either index can arguably be seen as a sign of a location's prominence. On the other hand, the limited scope of both indices suggests that locations not on the

---

5   More information on the Global Competitiveness Report is available at: www.weforum. org/issues/global-competitiveness (accessed 9 July 2012).

6   Further details on the index can be found at: http://www.atkearney.com/index.php/ Publications/foreign-direct-investment-confidence-index.html (accessed 9 July 2012).

7   For further details on Anholt-GfK place branding research, visit: www.gfkamerica.com/ practice_areas/roper_pam/placebranding/index.en.html (accessed 9 July 2012).

list may still have plenty in the way of investment attributes, therefore these indices should not be examined in isolation by potential investors.

fDi Intelligence's Cities and Regions of the Future

The Cities and Regions of the Future series is developed by fDi Intelligence, a division of the *Financial Times*. Unlike many other rankings, this series is open to submissions from economic development organisations, municipalities and governments, giving the rankings an awards-oriented nature. Cities and regions' submissions are reviewed against the following factors: economic potential, cost-effectiveness, human resources, quality of life, infrastructure, business-friendliness and FDI promotion. While some question the robustness of these and other award-oriented rankings, the initiative's association with the *Financial Times* nevertheless lends it a degree of credibility and prominence among corporate leaders, which is a reason in its own right to attach importance to the series.

Newsweek's Best Countries in the World

Newsweek provides an interactive online tool which ranks 100 countries on the basis of five factors: economic dynamism (the openness of a country's economy and the breadth of its corporate sector), education, health, political environment and quality of life.[8] Given the sheer mass of data available to investors and other corporate leaders, presentation can play an important role alongside the actual content and methodology. That said, to give a ranking such a seemingly subjective and even simplistic title as 'Best Countries in the World' does arguably bring the ranking's methodological robustness somewhat into question.

Economist Intelligence Unit's Liveability Ranking Report

The Economist Intelligence Unit (EIU) Liveability Ranking assesses 140 cities around the world on their living conditions. Each city is assessed for its strengths or weaknesses relating to over 30 quantitative and qualitative factors that fit into five broad categories: stability, healthcare, culture and environment, education and infrastructure. Each of the 30 factors is rated as acceptable, tolerable, uncomfortable, undesirable or intolerable, and the scores are then compiled to give a score out of 100 (where 100 is considered

---

8   Newsweek's interactive infographic can be explored here: http://www.thedailybeast. com/newsweek/2010/08/15/interactive-infographic-of-the-worlds-best-countries.html (accessed 9 July 2012).

ideal).[9] There is some disagreement about the level of importance investors (and therefore economic development organisations) should place on quality of life indices. Some believe that it should come quite far down the list of priorities, and that factors such as the operational environment, availability of talent and market potential are of far greater importance than whether a city is an enjoyable place to live in. For FDI projects which are heavily dependent on executive relocation, knowledge transfer and capacity-building in new markets, however, quality of life is arguably a key factor in persuading top talent to relocate and spearhead those projects.

Global Peace Index

Run by the Institute for Economics and Peace, the Global Peace Index is compiled using 23 indicators which range from a country's military expenditure levels to its relations with neighbouring countries and the level of respect for human rights. The index's aim is: 'to provide a quantitative measure of peacefulness, comparable over time, that will provide a greater understanding of the mechanisms that nurture and sustain peace'. While the index is deemed by some to have limited immediate relevance for investment, the social upheavals and other spates of violence witnessed in 2011, especially across the Middle East, serve as a potent reminder that civil unrest and violence can serve as a strong disincentive to invest, particularly in an uncertain economic climate. The index's sophisticated, interactive format also makes it a user-friendly online tool whose reputation and prominence has grown in recent years.[10]

Economic Freedom Index

The Heritage Foundation's Economic Freedom Index, drawn up in partnership with the *Wall Street Journal*, creates ten benchmarks that gauge the economic freedom of 184 countries around the world: business freedom, trade freedom, fiscal freedom, government spending, monetary freedom, investment freedom, financial freedom, property rights, freedom from corruption and labour freedom.[11] This index is particularly important to note when targeting US audiences, since both the Heritage Foundation and the *Wall Street Journal* are broadly well-regarded commentators in the country.

---

9   Further information on the methodology used by the EIU in compiling the Liveability Ranking, as well as the results of its August 2011 survey, can be found at: http://www.eiu.com/public/topical_report.aspx?campaignid=liveabilityAug2011 (accessed 9 July 2012).

10 For more information and to explore the Global Peace Index, visit: www.visionofhumanity.org (accessed 9 July 2012).

11 Further information available at: http://www.heritage.org/index/about (accessed 9 July 2012).

These and other indices, while viewed by some economic development professionals with a degree of cynicism, are nevertheless reviewed by many investors, and therefore need to be taken into consideration and understood. One could even argue that the methodology they employ is less important than the influence they have among their readers, although understanding the former is necessary if a location is going to be able to competently respond to their findings. Only in this way will locations be able to engage in a compelling dialogue with investors and explain to them how a particular ranking or result either is or isn't relevant to their specific investment plans, or doesn't paint a complete or even true picture of the realities they will encounter.

Joining the club: South Africa's accession to the BRICS was widely seen as a diplomatic triumph. Signs also suggest it will bolster and sustain the country's recent encouraging FDI rebound

Source: Ministry of External Affairs of India.

5 Politics and Public Diplomacy

Interest does not tie nations together; it sometimes separates them.
But sympathy and understanding does unite them.

Woodrow Wilson

In an increasingly commercialised and globalised world, the degree of influence exerted by international politics on day-to-day FDI can somewhat be brought into question. It certainly tends to be the driving force behind protectionist measures, as we have seen in Chapter 3. When it comes to championing and promoting FDI, however, how much of a bearing do political dealings truly have on the outcome?

A GOVERNMENT'S ROLES AND LIMITS

When British Prime Minister David Cameron visited China on a trade mission in November 2010, he boldly claimed that the UK government was 'working to agree a new target to double the value of [its] bilateral trade with China by 2015'. His statement raises interesting questions about the role of governments in setting and implementing targets in an area such as trade. As economists and other influential commentators stated at the time of this trade mission, trade and investment is first and foremost brought about through interactions between individuals and companies, rather than governments, diplomats and civil servants, although the latter clearly have an important role to play in eliminating trade and investment barriers as well as negotiating with their international counterparts on the myriad of policy areas that affect trade and investment, from monetary policy to bilateral and multilateral free trade agreements. When it comes to trade and investment, a government's role should first and foremost be that of an enabler or facilitator, rather than the primary 'driver'.

There are two important exceptions to this rule, however, and these relate to state-owned assets (the FDI target) and state-driven investments (the FDI source), where international political and diplomatic relations can clearly play an important role. When the two come together in one investment project, the matter can become highly politicised, as evidenced by the case of Dubai Ports World we reviewed in Chapter 3, and with sovereign wealth funds and other state-controlled investment bodies forming an increasingly important source of much-needed investment, international politics and FDI certainly cannot be dissociated.

BP's recent ventures – and difficulties – in Russia serve as a potent reminder of the important role politics can play in FDI, especially when it comes to hampering investment. When BP signed an agreement with AAR, a consortium of Russian billionaires, in 2003, thus forming the joint venture TNK-BP, the deal was greeted enthusiastically by shareholders and political leaders alike: the British energy giant had high hopes that the close ties to the Kremlin held by some of AAR's members would be of great benefit to the development of the company's activities in Russia. For its part, AAR saw great advantage in the technical and management knowledge transfer and capacity-building the venture would bring. By 2007, however, it had become apparent that the two sides had very different visions for the joint venture. AAR's consortium members had seen the alliance as a means of turning a part-Russian energy company into a truly global player with the help of BP's international expertise. BP, on the other hand, was keen to limit the joint venture's activities to within the confines of Russia and the CIS – after all, its expansion into other key energy markets would only have led to the creation of a competitor to BP's fully owned operations. BP's reluctance to take the company beyond Russia's borders was also frowned upon by Vladimir Putin and his administration at a time when Russian policy was highly in favour of corporate expansions abroad. This may go some way to explaining the lack of support the Russian government has given BP in its major disputes with AAR in recent years, and most significantly relating to the planned joint venture with Rosneft announced in January 2011. AAR opposed the venture on the grounds that it broke an exclusivity clause signed between BP and AAR back in 2003. The newly proposed venture subsequently collapsed, and in late 2011 Rosneft finally selected ExxonMobil as its joint venture partner.

BP's foiled attempt to forge a partnership with Rosneft is not the result of direct governmental intervention or protectionism (Rosneft is a state-controlled company, after all). But there is little doubt that the privileged connections the AAR consortium's members had with the Kremlin and other key areas of the Russian political establishment put BP in a considerably weaker negotiating position when this dispute came to the foreground. It serves as a potent reminder of Russia's top-heavy balance of power, and that if corporations are to succeed in the country, then privileged contacts with Russia's leadership are important – especially when the going gets tough.

The politicisation of proposed investment deals is by no means confined to dealing in emerging markets like Russia, however. The year 2011 also witnessed a major political dispute relating to a proposed investment between two of the founding members of the EU (currently the world's most integrated multinational union). The proposed investor was France's dairy giant Lactalis, while the target was Italy's largest milk products manufacturer, Parmalat. The protectionist instincts this proposed deal ignited among Italian politicians during March–June 2011 cannot be viewed in isolation. Italy has a long history of being one of Europe's more open economies when it comes to foreign acquisitions, yet this deal came at a time when a series of French companies were seeking to acquire some of Italy's leading corporate icons. France's luxury goods giant LVMH had acquired a controlling stake in Italy's jewellery group Bulgari in March that year; BNP Paribas was also reported to be interested in Banca Popolare di Milano, and it was looking increasingly likely that France's EDF would ultimately acquire Edison, Italy's second-largest power group (which it ultimately did go on to acquire in December 2011). With so many bilateral – and crucially, mono-directional – acquisitions in the pipeline, it was arguably inevitable that emotions in Italy's parliament would run high and political rhetoric become vociferous. Objections to the Parmalat deal were not confined to the backbenches or political sidelines, either: Guilio Tremonti, Italy's Economy Minister, declared he would seek a way to keep the firm in Italian hands, potentially through creating a national consortium to counter Lactalis's bid. The government also sought to implement new rules that would protect strategic firms from foreign takeovers.

Italy's vehement defence of Parmalat was grounded in principles that went beyond concerns of a French acquisition spree, however. Firstly, and most obviously, the country was facing increased economic instability and a weak centre-right coalition government whose leader, Silvio Berlusconi, had been embroiled in a series of scandals. The coalition was therefore eager to score political points with an increasingly sceptical public by being seen to protect Italian jobs from foreign takeovers (this concern being accentuated by the fact that Lactalis already had a reputation as a tough negotiator). The second key driver behind Italy's resistance to the proposed takeover was Parmalat's specific recent history. In 2003, Parmalat was facing bankruptcy in the wake of a major accounting fraud that had led some to name the troubled company

'Europe's Enron'. The Italian government had played a key role in saving the firm and sending it on the road to recovery; as such, it was unsurprising that an acquisition attempt from a firm whose home country was known for its own protectionist measures would be met with hostility.

In spite of Italy's objections, the deal ultimately went ahead, due in part to a bilateral Franco-Italian summit in April 2011 which eased strained relations between the two countries. In addition, Italy's trade unions ended up supporting the proposed deal when Lactalis pledged not to shed jobs, and to retain the group's headquarters in Italy. Crucially, the European Commission also lent its approval to the proposed takeover in mid-June, declaring that the deal 'would not significantly impede effective competition in Italy or any other European Economic Area (EEA) countries'.[1] This judgment paved the way to the €3.4 billion takeover bid which took place on 8 July that year, making Lactalis the world's number one dairy products company.

72

This highly publicised investment deal took place within the relatively safe haven of the EU, where a plethora of community-wide legislation is in place to challenge trade and investment barriers that have no, little or questionable justification and that hinder the functioning of the EU's single market. Companies looking at intra-EU investments can therefore draw comfort from cases such as Lactalis and Parmalat and the legislative provisions supporting them.

Some important lessons can also be learned from this particular case, however. Many of those pertaining to protectionism can be found in the suggested considerations and measures outlined in Chapter 3. However, this case also reveals a couple of additional learning points that should be borne in mind, and especially by would-be investors who won't necessarily have the legislative provisions of the EU or another deeply integrated economic union or community to rely on.

Firstly, investors should give consideration to other investment projects in the target country, either in the same sector, or as in the case of the Lactalis-Parmalat deal, from the same source country. Just as a series of planned foreign investments, and especially takeovers, in one sector of a given country can give cause for alarm (think of the UK's automotive industry, for example, and the investments that have been made by Indian, US and German firms over the past couple of decades), a series of planned investments or

---

1   The Commission's press release on the decision from 14 June 2011 can be viewed at:
     http://europa.eu/rapid/pressReleasesAction.do?reference=IP/11/701&format=HTML&a
     ged=1&language=EN&guiLanguage=en (accessed 18 August 2012).

takeovers from one country can give rise to concerns that the source country is snapping up the target country's prime assets, and may even be the manifestation of the former's commercial influence and even domination over the latter. We have seen such concerns come to the national and even international foreground not only in the Lactalis-Parmalat deal, but also in the case of Dubai Ports World which we examined in Chapter 2 – and these are only two examples of many such cases. Country-specific factors such as upcoming elections or the fragility of existing governments also need to be taken into consideration when investors are planning their investment strategies. Concerns over influence and domination in particular have important implications for emerging sources of investment such as SWFs and new corporate giants from high-growth markets, and this suggests that bilateral political relations are of great importance if bilateral trade and investment is also to thrive. In other words, while politics, diplomacy and international relations should not be the driver of FDI, an absence of political goodwill between given states can make FDI projects between them far harder to bring to fruition.

73

PUBLIC DIPLOMACY

Where politics and traditional diplomacy find their limitations when it comes to driving trade and investment, public diplomacy is quite a different matter. By its very nature, public diplomacy involves outreach and interaction with a broader public, and given the evident influence of public opinion on political decisions (including those that affect international investments), public diplomacy is increasingly being seen as a vital enabler of FDI as channels of communication open up and governments and their administrations connect directly with their international audiences through new platforms that add to those of traditional diplomacy and other official intermediaries such as chambers of commerce.

One country which effectively uses public diplomacy to support its international investment agenda and other political goals is South Africa. In Chapter 2 we looked at how the country's International Marketing Council is spearheading efforts to promote brand South Africa internationally. These efforts are not aimed only at international tourists, consumers and corporations, however: one of the IMC's key missions is to use state branding as a means of positioning the country in terms of its international relations objectives. As such, the IMC showcases a brand attribute rarely promoted by other countries in their branding efforts – that of an experienced and effective international mediator in challenging political disputes. In short, it is leveraging the principles of marketing to advance its foreign policy agenda and ensure the country has an important voice on the global stage. As Dr Jeremy Youde from the University of Minnesota Duluth effectively summarised, South Africa 'promotes itself as having insights and abilities not possessed by other potential mediators, thus distinguishing its "brand" from competing "products"'.[2] The IMC has pursued an ambitious agenda to respond to this objective over the past decade: in 2004, for example, copies of *Time* magazine distributed to delegates at the World Economic Forum were wrapped in advertising from the IMC. The key message of this advertisement, which was subsequently named by *Economist* as one of the ten most memorable, was that South Africa was capable of resolving international conflicts by drawing on its own recent experience of ending apartheid. This was accompanied in the following years by a TV documentary, workshops, media visits and a host of other activities all aimed at telling leaders and influencers around the world what South Africa was doing – and achieving – as an international mediator and peace broker in the emerging yet still deeply troubled continent of Africa.

ON TOP OF THE GAME

The year 2010 was a pivotal one for South Africa, and not least in terms of its international standing and diplomatic achievements. In hosting the FIFA World Cup, South Africa clearly demonstrated that it was a global player capable of hosting a world-class event. The World Cup's impact and implications went far beyond the event, however: it marked a celebration of sustained and positive change in South Africa's recent economic and political history. A formerly segregated nation was now rallying its enthused citizens and people from around the world to come together in celebration of sport. If South Africa was looking for its ultimate brand enhancer and an opportunity to showcase itself to the world, then the World Cup provided that golden opportunity. Later that year, the continent's largest and most developed economy secured another economic and diplomatic triumph – it was invited to join the now infamous BRIC group of large emerging economies, following an intense diplomatic agenda which saw South Africa's President Jacob Zuma visit each of the BRIC countries that year. The invitation was officially made in December 2010 by the Chinese government, which at that time held the rotating chairmanship of the group, and in April 2011 South Africa joined the group's third summit meeting in China.

Not everyone agreed with this move – perhaps most significantly, the man who coined the term 'BRIC' back in 2003: Jim O'Neill from Goldman Sachs.

2   'Selling the State: State Branding as a Political Resource in South Africa', Jeremy Youde, *Place Branding and Public Diplomacy*, vol. 5, no. 2, May 2009, p. 134.

When the announcement of South Africa's membership was made in December 2010, O'Neill commented that the deal 'made no sense' to him. How was it that far larger emerging economies such as Mexico, South Korea and Turkey were not being invited to join this prestigious group? Part of the answer undoubtedly lies in the considerable interest China and other BRIC economies have not only in South Africa's natural resources, but those of Africa more broadly. As such, President Zuma's tactical positioning of South Africa as a gateway to the continent throughout South Africa's series of BRIC visits will undoubtedly have strengthened – and perhaps even made – the case for the country's subsequent membership.

The significance of being admitted to this club cannot be underestimated. Even as investors now increasingly look to newer informal country groupings such as the N11 ('Next 11')[3] or the CIVETS (Columbia, Indonesia, Vietnam, Egypt, Turkey and South Africa), the BRICS, as they are now known following South Africa's admission to the group, will still remain at the heart of the global FDI agenda for years, and most probably decades, to come. A.T. Kearney's 2012 FDI Confidence Index is a testament to the BRICS' enduring attractiveness; China, India and Brazil take the top three spots in the index, while South Africa and Russia take eleventh and twelfth place respectively.[4] For South Africa, this represents a major rebound from 2010, when it didn't even feature in the top 25 list, and while 2010 FDI inflows were down on 2008 and 2009 following the country's slide into recession, there are now strong signs of renewed investor interest, not only in the country's abundant natural resources, but also automotive, chemicals and retail sectors.

IN THE SPOTLIGHT AND UNDER THE MICROSCOPE

South Africa's recent concerted efforts in traditional and public diplomacy are paying dividends when it comes to the country's investment prospects. The World Cup was a prime example of an event and brand catalyst that doesn't just put its host country in the spotlight – it puts it under the microscope, too. While world events such as these are opportunities to showcase a country's achievements, they can also reveal its shortcomings. Think of the criticism various international political leaders and other influencers voiced over China's human rights record in the run-up to and during the 2008 Olympic Games hosted by Beijing. As we saw in Chapter 1, poor standards in Indian infrastructure received global attention when only weeks before the Commonwealth Games hosted in Delhi, shocking images of insalubrious accommodation for the

---

3 The 'Next 11' countries are: Bangladesh, Egypt, Indonesia, Iran, Mexico, Nigeria, Pakistan, Philippines, South Korea, Turkey and Vietnam.
4 *Cautious Investors Feed a Tentative Recovery.*

athletes, and more tragically, a collapsed footbridge which injured 23 people, spread globally and solicited widespread condemnation.

Events such as these remind us that for all the efforts a country may make in both traditional and public diplomacy, we now live in age of enforced transparency where the idea that a government or its administration can singularly own its country's brand image through mono-directional marketing, or can run its diplomatic agenda safe in the knowledge that discretion and confidentiality will not be breached, is fading fast. The WikiLeaks controversy which exploded onto the world stage in late 2010 demonstrated the extent to which leaked confidential cables could shake diplomatic ties, with all the potential implications for FDI these and future exposures could entail. Meanwhile, the proliferation of social media means that public diplomacy and place branding efforts need to take account of – and crucially, engage with – a broader and vocally empowered set of stakeholders through an ever-expanding number of online platforms.

Chapter 6 provides a more detailed examination of how the proliferation of data and the digital empowerment of stakeholders is changing the way both investors and economic development organisations approach FDI. As the global economy teeters on the dividing line between economic uncertainty and a cautious recovery, what medium- to longer-term FDI prospects can be expected, and what can economic developers do to optimise opportunities and minimise risk?

Designed in Africa: The future FDI landscape will be increasingly digital and mobile, but the west does not hold a monopoly on innovation. The Way-C tablet, pictured above, was designed in the Congo and has been widely hailed as 'Africa's answer to the iPad'
Source: VMK Plc.

6 Where Next for FDI?

We've kind of taken for granted that people will want to come here, and we aren't out there hungry, selling America and trying to attract new business into America.

Barack Obama, Hawaii, November 2011

Most statistical data sets, surveys, indices and anecdotal evidence suggest that the global FDI landscape is now formed by a somewhat ambiguous mix of cautious optimism and unwavering uncertainty. The bar charts are starting to rise again, businesses leaders increasingly speak of the need to seek out new markets, and yet issues such as the eurozone sovereign debt crisis and uprisings and tensions in the Middle East serve as a potent reminder of the world's enduring instabilities. In the midst of such instabilities, corporate investors are now seeking to navigate their courses to sustainable growth. While the seas may be rougher, the skies are undoubtedly clearer, thanks to unprecedented levels of data, transparency and interconnectivity. All of these factors mean that economic development organisations need to become smart and focused when it comes to identifying which sectors and companies to target, and how to engage with them.

WELCOME TO THE AGE OF HYPER-CONNECTIVITY AND ENFORCED TRANSPARENCY

Chapter 5 referred to this age of 'enforced transparency' brought about by the rise of social media in the past five years. The proliferation of data and conversations that flow through a multitude of online channels and platforms now means the old adage that what others say about you is more important than what you say about yourself has never been more pertinent. This notion, and the accompanying decline of the concept of 'brand ownership', has clearly been demonstrated time and again in the corporate world over the past few years, and therefore entails some important implications for international investors as they seek to build or uphold their reputations in foreign markets. One of the most dramatic recent examples of how these changing forces can have a bearing on a company's reputation can be seen in the 2010 Deepwater Horizon disaster in the Gulf of Mexico. This tragedy presented the protagonist, BP, with nothing short of an equally large PR disaster. In spite of the company's efforts to engage stakeholders and keep them informed of the clean-up operation and other measures, vocal critics managed to reduce these efforts to a comparative squeak: the company's Twitter campaign versus that of a satirical spoof account set up under the name 'BPGlobalPR' was the ultimate proof that the company was not only no longer in full control of its brand, but that this brand had even been hijacked. Furthermore, this spoof account was attracting nearly five times the number of followers as BP America's official Twitter account.

So where do such developments leave locations – and more specifically, economic development and investment promotion bodies? From a reactive and defensive standpoint, the good news is that locations, unlike companies, have long been accustomed to the idea that a multitude of stakeholder groups shape and display their brands – while a location's brand can and should be managed effectively, it cannot be owned. Investment promotion, by its very definition, is a proactive exercise, however, so the question that needs to be addressed is: to what extent can social media help to generate investment leads for a location?

There are plenty of statistics and several anecdotal examples to make the case for implementing a social media strategy as an integral part of an investment promotion campaign. At a broad corporate level, Unisfair, the virtual events company, conducted a marketing survey in 2010 where it asked 500 technology marketing professionals what they considered to be the top lead-generation channels. As Figure 6.1 illustrates, social media was by far the most popular channel, followed by virtual events and mobile. When it comes to specific platforms within the social media landscape, the 2011 *State of Inbound Marketing Report* by the online marketing company HubSpot found that LinkedIn and company blogs were the most effective platforms when it actually came to acquiring a customer through the use of social media, followed by Facebook and Twitter (see Figure 6.2).

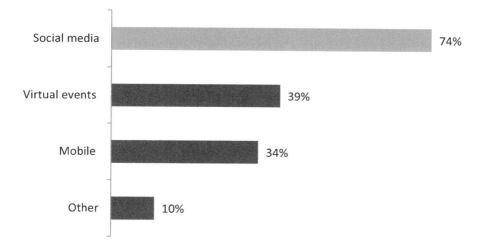

Figure 6.1   Top lead-generation channels
Source: Unisfair Marketing Survey, 25 May 2010. Respondents: 500 technology
marketing professionals. Graph courtesy of HubSpot.

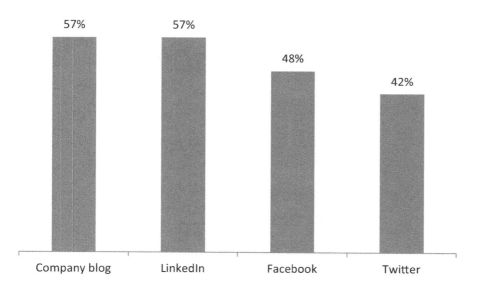

Figure 6.2   Channels for acquiring a customer
Source: *State of Inbound Marketing Report*, HubSpot, 2011.

The economic development and investment promotion world is increasingly
embracing social media, too. The initial hype has subsided and there are
increasing examples of agencies that are effectively using channels to
generate investment leads (a couple of which we'll examine later). Yet recent

evidence suggests that there's still some degree of scepticism or hesitation when it comes to social media. A recent survey sponsored by the US-based International Economic Development Council (IEDC) asked more than 300 members about their use of social media – the results indicated that social media is still a relatively 'new medium' for economic developers.

However, the question economic developers should be asking is whether social media is such a new channel for the corporate audiences they're trying to reach. Are today's corporate decision-makers and their influencers 'digital natives', and if not, what is the likelihood that the corporations' next generation of leaders will be? Economic developers should take the changing landscape of how corporate audiences digest information and interact online as an opportunity to take the lead.

So how can an organisation organise its efforts and adopt an optimal approach to social media for lead-generation? Figure 6.3 illustrates a cumulative and repetitive process. We will then explore each element in detail.

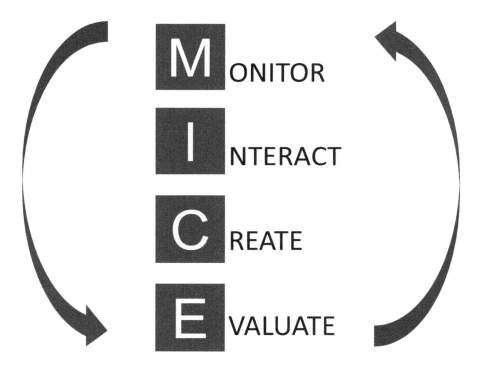

Figure 6.3   The MICE approach to social media

Monitor

You firstly need to monitor closely what is being said about you online, by whom, and where, before you can decide how best to engage with these audiences. There are plenty of tools and sites you can use to monitor conversations about or involving your organisation or key topics, and the number of these monitoring tools is growing constantly. Here are a few examples of free tools that are worth taking a look at and trialling:

- Addict-o-matic (www.addictomatic.com) is a multi-channel platform that enables you to build a custom page and follow the latest buzz on a given topic.

- Twilert (www.twilert.com) is a service which provides regular email alerts of tweets containing references to your organisation.

- Monitter (www.monitter.com) is a real-time, live Twitter search and monitoring tool which allows you to combine multiple search terms, with results coming up simultaneously on one screen.

- Blogdigger (www.blogdigger.com) is a leading blog search engine.

In addition, setting up Google Alerts and conducting regular searches on Twitter are effective ways to track content and conversations.

Interact and Create

Once you know what is being said about you, by whom, and on which platforms, you then need to interact with your audiences by creating, sharing and discussing content. In a recent survey of business-to-business (B2B) buyers, 85 per cent of respondents said they want B2B vendors to engage and interact with them online. There's no reason to suggest this would be any different in government-to-business collaboration (where the target audience remains on the business side).

The first and most important point to remember is that social networking – just like professional network- and relationship-building – doesn't happen overnight: it takes time, effort and commitment. You need to leverage your online advocates and ambassadors to build new relationships, while the proliferation of online content and data means the content you share has to be helpful and interesting for the intended audience. When an investor expresses an interest in your location via a social network, try to move this engagement onto a traditional, more exclusive channel (for example, email or a phone call) as soon as possible – like any form of networking, the initial conversation may take place in an open forum, but when it comes down to discussing details, this is best done privately.

Evaluate

Finally, you need to make sure that you're constantly evaluating your social media activities, and in order to do this, it's important to have the right metrics in place. Firstly, it's not all about the number of followers, group members or blog hits you have. While *quantity* matters if you want your social media efforts to have any meaningful impact, the *quality* of your content matters far more. Here are some questions you should be asking about your social media activities:

- Are you focusing your efforts on the right platforms?

- Are you connecting with the right people in your pipeline or on your list of targets?

- What level of audience engagement have you seen? Are meaningful conversations developing, or are you talking into a silent abyss?

- Have any promising leads come about, either through or with the help of social media engagement?

- Have any of these leads translated into investment projects?

Now that we've looked at what should be done, let's consider what not to do when using social media. Here are some common pitfalls to avoid.

Don't Just Broadcast

Social media should not be seen solely as a channel for you to broadcast, market and sell your attributes. Social media is about creating meaningful conversations and sharing content that adds value to followers and members. If you're only in it for the hard sell, people will soon lose interest.

Don't Adopt a Half-hearted Approach

Social media engagement needs constant, ongoing effort. If you only see social media as a means of placing ad-hoc posts 'when you have the time', again people will soon lose interest. After all, if you arranged a networking event where there were extended periods of silence and no content, people might become bored and leave. The same applies to social media platforms – just look at how often people 'defriend' on Facebook or 'unfollow' on Twitter. You need people who can commit to monitoring and engaging with online audiences and who don't see it as a burdensome addition to their heavy workload. Think about what a dormant social media platform would look like to a prospect – it's arguably as bad as having a seriously outdated website. Furthermore, it should be remembered that social media are far less costly than traditional marketing initiatives like advertising, printed publications and event hosting.

Don't Be Predictable

Vary the format of your updates – use text, share links, documents videos and photos. Make statements, but also ask open questions. Keep things fresh. Updates that are predictable, boring or annoying undermine the relationship with your followers.

Don't Try to Be Everywhere, Following Everyone

Just because you follow someone, don't expect them to follow you back! Trying to follow anyone and everyone in the hope of building up your numbers won't get you far without good, relevant content – and besides, it dilutes your efforts. You need to know where your audience is, and focus on these channels.

One Size Does Not Fit All

It can be easy to become focused on leading social media tools like Twitter, LinkedIn and Facebook, all of which dominate in the English-speaking world, and forget that there are a host of other highly popular networks out there, many with several millions of members. Continental Europe, for example, has a highly diverse social media landscape which includes international networks such Xing and Viadeo, as well as national networks which are leaders in a given country, such as Hungary's iWiW and Russia's vkontakte. In China, the leading business social network at the time of writing was Tianji (owned by Viadeo), with over seven million registered users. Meanwhile, Orkut (which is owned by Google) remains a leading social network in both Brazil and India.

Economic developers need to ensure that their lead-generation efforts are targeted and relevant to the market (or markets) in question. Enterprise Florida, for example, has made effective use of its Viadeo profile and group for the French market through growing its network and members of the group.

A number of prospects have been identified via the group, and the agency has even successfully secured investment from the group's membership.

At a broader level, the social media efforts of organisations like UK Trade & Investment (UKTI) have also paid significant dividends when it comes to profiling and investment attraction. UKTI's Twitter and LinkedIn groups are growing constantly (at the time of writing, the latter was adding an average of more than 100 members per week), while the social media content comes in a variety of formats, from videos to blog posts to questions to reports. So what has the impact been? In the past couple of years, the company's social media activities have been one of the key drivers of traffic to the main UKTI website (Twitter alone has been the second highest referrer of traffic). This has helped result in a major boost in investor enquiries, and in 2011, the UK received a higher number of investment projects than any other country in Europe.

MORE FOCUSED, AND MORE ENGAGED

The principles of engaging and adopting a targeted approach are not limited to the domain of social media. Long before LinkedIn and Twitter took the communications world by storm, calls were being made by investors and consultants alike for a more targeted approach to investment promotion. Destination marketing and place branding, for example, are still widely regarded as one of an investment promotion agency's core roles, and in Chapter 2 we examined how brands, when built and promoted correctly, can act as significant bases and even guarantors for investment. However, as the FDI landscape becomes ever more crowded and competitive, companies are now primarily on the look-out for locations that don't only sell and promote credentials, but solutions, too. This has led to the rise of what is commonly referred to as *proposition-based marketing*, where rather than talking about generic investment attributes and other relevant credentials, investment promotion agencies develop sector-specific value propositions that outline how their locations can add tangible benefits to a would-be investor, and how they differ advantageously from competing locations. As such, value propositions are more business solutions than location solutions, and the development of these can then place the investment promotion agency in a strong position to develop unique selling points and propositions targeted at specific companies. These are important in a global investment environment where companies seek specialist sector expertise in their target locations: it's all well and good having the right mix of location attributes, but if investment promotion agencies aren't presenting these in an appropriate, tailored and compelling way, or showing themselves to be reliable partners who understand the company and will fully help it establish its project in the optimal way, then they risk missing out on potentially important opportunities.

In order to build these value propositions effectively, agencies need to understand and use three core building blocks as their base:

1. **the demand-driven characteristics** and investor motives for expanding abroad;

2. **the supply-side characteristics** of that location in general, as well as the specific services offered by the agency;

3. **a comparative analysis** which benchmarks that location against all of its competitors for a particular sector or even a future planned project.

It is also important that these activities are conducted in tandem with the location-identification and decision-making processes of a given company. This clearly requires direct engagement with companies.

So what are typically the most effective ways to target companies? Direct engagement, whether through emails and telephone calls, in person at conferences and other events, or through social networking, has time and again been proven to yield more and better investment leads. As part of these engagement efforts, it is important that agencies make it clear to investors that they were not contacted at random, that preliminary research has been conducted by the agency to understand the company's business and its needs, and finally, that a business proposal can be made with regard to the needs identified.

To put it simply, proposition-based marketing and effective investor targeting need to be less about the location, and more about the investor.

THE BATTLEGROUND FOR MOBILE TALENT

In Chapter 4, we looked at talent as one of the key factors influencing a company's decision of whether and where to locate its investment project. An increasingly mobile and transnationally minded young workforce means that competition to attract and retain talented workers has never been greater – and this applies to locations as much as it does corporations. This talented workforce is not only 'mobile' in the physical sense of the word; ever more sophisticated smartphones and tablets with endless apps and ever-growing data packages mean that the young and rising talent of today are hyper-connected 'digital natives'. This connection and engagement with a seemingly infinite number of peer-to-peer channels and forums means that investment promotion agencies need to be fully engaged not only with the corporations they seek to attract, but also the talented workers these corporations in turn employ (or are seeking to employ). Part of this engagement can, of course, take place through social networks and other online channels, but it shouldn't stop there. Much in the same way as economic development organisations attend trade shows and other outbound missions, agencies should also consider how to adopt a similar approach to identifying and attracting talent. Montréal International, for example, views attracting FDI and talent as 'complementary activities that feed each other, creating a virtuous circle'.[1] Montréal International has been organising a series of international recruiting missions on behalf of Greater Montréal's businesses – these have involved targeting both specific sectors and geographies. The organisation also has a social media programme in place to promote the advantages of working and living in the Greater Montréal area.

Table 6.1   The link between FDI, talent and brand

Top 10 Cities for Inward FDI 2010–11*	Location Talent Indicator**	A.T. Kearney Global Cities Index Rank 2010
1. Singapore	Top 30 global university	8th
2. London	2 top 10 global universities	2nd
3. Shanghai	Top 100 global university	21st
4. Dubai	Leading regional industry clusters	27th
5. Hong Kong	Top 25 global university	5th
6. Beijing	Top 50 global university	15th
7. New York	Top 10 global university	1st
8. Paris	Top 35 global university	4th
9. Bangalore	Leading IT centre of excellence	58th
10. Sydney	Top 40 global university	9th

Source: OCO Global.

*Note*s:

*   Data from fDi Markets.

**   Universities data provided by QS World University Rankings 2011/12.

---

1   Jacques St-Laurent, President and CEO, Montréal International, commenting in his contribution to OCO's *Annual Report 2011/12*, 'Generation Mobile: Securing Top Talent for FDI', October 2011.

Recent research by the economic development consultancy OCO found a strong correlation between leading destination brands, the presence of top global universities and centres of excellence, and leading FDI hotspots (see Table 6.1). The big winners in this battleground tend to be world-class cities that have the right combination of buzz and promise to attract top talent. This clearly has implications for second-tier cities and more rural regions that need to carve out their own niches in terms of talent and investor propositions.

Fortunately, there are other forces at play which mean that the top global cities are not the only beneficiaries of this increasingly mobile talent – the past couple of years have seen an unprecedented number of talented workers from emerging markets returning home.[2]

In Africa, many of the continent's economic powerhouses like Nigeria, Ghana and South Africa are now witnessing unprecedented brain gains, fuelled largely by returning diaspora keen to be a part of their countries' success stories and economic growth. In South Africa, The Homecoming Revolution, an NGO dedicated to engaging with diaspora in key developed countries and encouraging them to return home, has built up a network of more than 20,000 expatriates, while a recent survey commissioned by Reconnect Africa (an online business news portal aimed at Africans overseas) showed that a third of professionals of African origin currently working in the West see better opportunities for career progression in Africa. Whether this will translate into a pan-continental brain gain for Africa remains to be seen, and a shortage of skilled talent remains an impediment to Africa's economic development. However, certain countries have seen a huge influx of returning diaspora: during 2009–10, more than 10,000 Nigerian expatriates were reported to have returned home, while data from the International Office for Migration (IOM) reveals that of more than 1.1 million Ghanaians that emigrated during 2000–2007, only 153,000 did not return.

The stories behind each mass repatriation are varied, but a common driver which comes up time and again is the realisation that ambitious young professionals can progress their careers far more rapidly back home than if they stay abroad. Many top young graduates leave already lucrative and promising careers in the West with the realisation that they can become CEOs of successful nascent companies and other organisations in their home countries by the time they reach 30. *Newsweek* featured the revealing story

---

2   The analysis of returning diaspora which follows is based on an article I wrote for the *Financial Times*'s *fDi Magazine*, entitled 'Bringing Them All Back Home', February/March 2012, pp. 94–5.

of one 30-year-old Harvard law graduate from Nigeria who turned down six-figure corporate job offers in the USA, choosing instead to return home in order to build and run a US$50 million private hospital with a charitable component for the poor.[3] This story and many others like it portray an important social and emotional dimension to these repatriations: talented African expatriates want to be a part of their countries' success stories and become leading agents of positive change in the continent.

Across the Atlantic Ocean, Latin America's prospects also appear to be brightening. The region's largest country, Brazil, will come into the global spotlight over the next four years thanks to the FIFA World Cup in 2014 and the Summer Olympics two years later. The build-up and staging of these two world-class events are set to symbolise the broader energy and promise of what is now the world's sixth largest economy (Brazil's economy was reported to have overtaken the UK's in 2011). All of this energy and promise has translated into a major influx of returning diaspora: Brazil's Justice Ministry recently estimated that around 2 million Brazilians now live abroad – a sharp decline since 2005, when the diaspora was estimated at around 4 million. It's not just broad notions of Brazil's promise and potential that are luring its expatriates back home, however: in 2010, research conducted into top executive pay by the Association of Executive Search Consultants (AESC) revealed that CEOs and directors of businesses based in São Paolo typically command higher salaries than their counterparts in New York, London, Singapore and Hong Kong. For this reason, talented Brazilians who once saw the traditional commercial centres of the USA, Europe and Asia as their best routes to a prosperous career are now seriously reconsidering their options.

Economic uncertainties in much of Europe and the continued growth of some markets in Central and Eastern Europe have also seemingly led to some interesting repatriation trends in recent years. The massive east–west migration spurred by the 2004 enlargement of the European Union is now showing signs of reversing as tens – and some estimate hundreds – of thousands of expatriates from Poland and other Central and Eastern European countries are leaving Western Europe to return home and pursue career opportunities more in line with their qualifications and experience. Many talented workers came to take jobs in the UK and elsewhere in Western Europe for which they were overqualified – for example, stories of Polish graduates and even junior white-collar workers who came to work as waiters or waitresses in London or plumbers in Paris were commonplace. Many other expatriates have of course pursued professional white-collar careers, too; but with stagnating economies and rising redundancies in the West contrasting with, for example, Poland's

---

3   'How Africa is Becoming the New Asia', pp. 44–6.

enduring economic growth (it is the only country in the EU not to have slipped into recession at some point since the onset of the 2008 financial crisis), many now see the appeal of returning home. Whatever jobs many of these returning expatriates came to pursue in the West, many have found that their international experience and exposure to new languages and cultures put them at a significant advantage when seeking employment back home.

The economic benefits of such brain gains are clear to see in many emerging markets. Renewed confidence among the Polish diaspora in their country's economic prospects also appears to correlate with foreign investor confidence in the country: in 2011, UNCTAD predicted that Poland will rank top in the EU for FDI during 2011–2013, based on the number of times a multinational company has referenced a country as a top FDI priority.

These returning diaspora do not constitute a panacea, however. In Brazil, for example, the elevated salaries of São Paolo's executives are in part driven by the scarcity of talent: even with Brazil's diaspora returning in their hundreds of thousands, the agency Manpower recently reported that 64 per cent of employers in Brazil encountered challenges in filling vacancies. With access to skilled labour increasingly being named as one of the top factors influencing an investment decision, addressing talent gaps will be of paramount importance if countries like Brazil are to reach their true economic and investment potential.

The same applies to Africa. While parts of the continent are displaying promising signs of economic development and talented diaspora continue returning in their droves, Africa's overall FDI performance has still been less than stellar of late (inflows to Africa continued to decline in 2011, albeit at a slower rate than in 2010). While many of the expatriates returning to Nigeria, for example, may be shining examples of highly educated, talented innovators, major challenges still remain when it comes to the calibre of the workforce at large. Take the World Economic Forum's 2011–2012 *Global Competitiveness Report* as one indication of these challenges: Nigeria ranked 114th out of 142 countries on higher education and training, while it came in at 127th position in the overall competitiveness index. One of the key challenges – and opportunities – facing countries like Nigeria is to ensure that the entrepreneurialism and innovation being injected into the economy by returning expatriates becomes a catalyst for broader investment in education, research and innovation – that way, such countries become not only places of returning talent, but emerging home-grown talent as well.

In spite of the challenges that lie ahead, the one thread these mass repatriations around the world have in common is that they display an undeniable sense of optimism among these returning diaspora about their countries' futures, an optimism which, if capitalised upon correctly, will in turn – it is hoped – lead to increasing levels of foreign investor confidence.

FDI, INNOVATION AND ENTREPRENEURIALISM: A SYMBIOTIC RELATIONSHIP

In Chapter 4 we looked at how leading global centres of excellence and innovation act as magnets for FDI – Tech City in London's East End and Medicon Valley in Scandinavia are two prime examples – but attracting FDI is far from the sole objective of such initiatives, nor will such a single-pronged approach necessarily deliver the best result for a location's economic development strategy. FDI is certainly one important strand in the economic development mix, but it should be complemented by initiatives to spur micro-entrepreneurialism, too.

In the run-up to the annual World Economic Forum's Davos gathering in 2012, the forum's founder, Professor Klaus Schwab, spoke of the need to address the worsening unemployment situation in various countries in Europe and elsewhere by moving 'from the pure concept of unemployment to the concept of micro-entrepreneurship'. Much in the same way that economic developers and other policymakers have spoken of the need to spend and invest our way out of recession or economic stagnation, we also need to look at innovating our way out of the current stagnant climate. We should not forget that some of the world's largest and most successful and innovative companies today began their lives in modest surroundings: Google started its life in a garage, while Facebook was set up in Mark Zuckerberg's university dorm.

Perhaps stories like these are what excite investors and policymakers about places like Tech City, which isn't just about outside investment and job creation, it's about entrepreneurial incubation and equipping today's up-and-coming digital innovators with the commercial skill sets they need to become tomorrow's tech leaders. For this reason, companies like Google and Cisco have been keen to invest in the creation of innovation centres in the area, while the British government provides support in the form of training and mentoring from industry veterans. Universities and other educational institutions also have a positive role to play in nurturing a spirit of entrepreneurialism among their students, and initiatives such as UCL and Imperial College's recent collaboration with Cisco to create a 'Future Cities Centre'[4] in Tech City are to

---

4   'Partnership with CISCO & Imperial in Tech City', http://www.ucl.ac.uk/enterprise/
     enterprise-news/cp-archive/citiesofthefuture, UCL Enterprise, 7 December 2011 (accessed
     9 July 2012).

be welcomed, as they provide an important space for businesses, academics and start-ups to collaborate openly in close proximity.

TODAY'S GREAT SCRAMBLE

At a macro level, there is no doubt that today's global FDI climate is driven by a great scramble. An ever-growing number of economic development organisations are now competing to attract and retain more cautious yet growth-seeking foreign investors, as well as an increasingly mobile and discerning talent base. The priorities for the former may often differ from the latter (for example, quality of life, often shunned as a 'nice-to-have' from a corporate perspective, tends to be far more important for individuals when considering where they and their families should build their lives). With access to talent often cited as one of the key drivers of FDI (see Figure 4.1), it is clear why many locations are tempted to promote their 'quality of life' credentials, but are they pitching these credentials to the right audience? Many promotional documents and videos are sent or presented to COOs or heads of global strategy in corporate headquarters thousands of miles away, yet more often than not, these people have no plans to move as part of their firm's foreign expansion. Furthermore, as we've seen with the rise of social media and peer-to-peer forums, a worker considering relocation is going to be far more influenced by advice and insight from trusted friends and acquaintances, as well as peer-to-peer platforms where uncensored information, opinions and photos can give a more revealing, realistic impression of a place than a glossy brochure, flash website or promotional YouTube video ever will.

What constitutes a scramble at the macro level should not translate into a scramble for investment at the individual organisational level, however. Economic development organisations need to be smart and targeted when it comes to their investment strategies. No location can be all things to everyone, and while a diversified economy is important for mitigating risks that come from sectors that are prone to cyclical downturns, economic developers need to be clear and honest about where their location's true competitive advantages lie.

With unemployment on the rise in many countries, the political pressure on economic developers to secure investments that lead to that commonly heard cry for 'jobs, jobs and more jobs' – whatever these may be – is often high. There are three reasons why this single-minded approach is typically the wrong one to follow:

1. The desirable sectors, business activities and corporations that are likely to truly add value to a location's sustainable economic development will increasingly be attracted to those sophisticated locations – and increasingly clusters – that make the perfect match for their business needs.

2. Locations that focus solely or primarily on their financial incentives and cost-related attributes run the risk of becoming magnets for cost reduction-seeking FDI and little else. There's the risk that many of the jobs created by these projects will be low-skilled, and as such will add little to the sustainable development of the location through knowledge transfer, and when another, cheaper market opens up or becomes more appealing, there's the risk that investors will simply pack up and move on.

3. Crucially, a quantity-driven scramble for FDI dilutes an organisation's efforts – not only in terms of investor attraction, but potentially investor retention, too. This is a potential danger for smaller organisations that don't have dedicated investor services and aftercare teams and where people are involved in the entire spectrum of activities – from marketing and lead identification right through to investor services, aftercare and development. In the scramble to attract new FDI, there's the risk that existing investors are not provided with the levels of service that they require or expect – this is a major oversight when, as we have seen, existing investors can often be the most powerful and compelling endorsers not only of the location, but also the economic development organisation itself.

FDI has been and is set to remain a great force for positive economic development throughout the world. The benefits it brings to national and local economies, as well as people's careers and professional development prospects, can be substantial.

For FDI to add significant, sustainable value to an economy, however, economic development organisations need to strike a careful balance between focusing on their strengths and supporting the development of a healthy, diversified economy. While a location may have strengths in sectors such as financial services, construction or real estate, there needs to be recognition that these and other sectors entail a degree of risk. Long-term growth sectors such as renewable energy, life sciences and digital media are often high on organisations' FDI wish-lists, therefore not everyone can necessarily get a slice of those particular 'FDI pies'.

To this end, there needs to be recognition that FDI is not a panacea. Economic growth and development should also come from within markets, so economic development organisations should be considering not only how they can attract FDI, but also how they can spur and nurture domestic innovation and entrepreneurialism, or at least partner more effectively with organisations mandated with this task.

We've seen that much of Africa, for example – seen by many as the 'final FDI frontier' – still has some way to go before it fulfils its sustainable FDI potential, both in terms of figures and ambition. In recent years, there has been much talk and excitement around how the Sahara Desert could unlock the solution for Europe's sustainable energy needs. Some go so far as to claim that the Sahara Desert could produce enough energy to power the entire European continent, but for the moment at least, such visions seem to bear little resemblance to reality. It takes a winning combination of boldness, vision – and, of course, financing on a massive scale – to make projects such as these feasible, yet we're already witnessing exciting, entrepreneurial developments in other sectors elsewhere in Africa. In January 2012, the Way-C tablet – commonly referred to as 'Africa's answer to the iPad' – was launched in the Congo.[5] It takes its name from an expression in a northern Congolese dialect meaning 'the light of the stars'. With an initial price tag of US$300, it is being marketed in ten countries in West Africa, as well as Belgium, France and India. Whether the Way-C tablet ultimately becomes a success and a credible competitor to the iPad in these markets remains to be seen, but this initiative and others like it are encouraging signs of Africa's entrepreneurial potential. This, coupled with a significant push on innovation and education, has the potential to unlock the door to a swathe of sustainable FDI in the continent.

One place's opportunity can, of course, be another place's potential threat, and other economies around the world will need to find their competitive niche in the evolving world order. A scramble suggests excitement, and for many places, this will mean pursuing and nurturing constant innovation and entrepreneurialism that harnesses that excitement.

---

5   'Way-C Tablet, the First African iPad Rival, Goes On Sale in Congo', Erin Conway-Smith, globalpost, http://www.globalpost.com/dispatches/globalpost-blogs/weird-wide-web/african-ipad-way-c-tablet-congo-verone-mankou, 30 January 2012 (accessed 9 July 2012).

Bibliography

BBC World Service Country Rating Poll, BBC, March 2011.

'Bringing Them All Back Home', Daniel Nicholls, *fDi Magazine*, February/ March 2012, pp. 94–5.

'Buffett Says India Insurance Ownership Limit Deters Berkshire Investment', Pooja Thakur and Jay Shankar, Bloomberg, http://www.bloomberg.com/ news/2011-03-23/buffett-says-india-insurance-ownership-limit-deters-investment.html, 23 March 2011 (accessed 9 July 2012).

Cautious Investors Feed a Tentative Recovery: The 2012 A.T. Kearney FDI Confidence Index, A.T. Kearney, November 2011.

'Chinese Protectionism Not the Yuan is Our Greatest Concern', Peter Foster, *The Telegraph*, http://www.telegraph.co.uk/finance/china-business/7764019/Chinese-protectionism-not-the-yuan-is-our-greatest-concern-says-top-US-negotiator.html, 25 May 2010 (accessed 9 July 2012).

Competing for Growth: How Business is Growing Beyond Boundaries, Ernst & Young, April 2011.

Competitive Identity: The New Brand Management for Nations, Cities and Regions, Simon Anholt, Palgrave Macmillan, 2007.

Country Brand Index 2010, FutureBrand (in partnership with BBC World News), November 2010.

Dead Aid: Why Aid is Not Working and How There is Another Way for Africa, Dambisa Moyo, Penguin, 2010.

Débâcle: The 11th GTA Report on Protectionism, Centre for Economic Policy Research, June 2012

Doing Business 2011, World Bank Group, November 2010.

Doing Business 2012, World Bank Group, October 2011.

Enter the Dragon – How China will Impact Europe's Renewable Energy Landscape, Taylor Wessing, October 2011

FDI Kaizen: Economic Development in a Leaner World, OCO Global Annual Report 2010/2011.

FDI Protectionism is On the Rise, Karl P. Sauvant, The World Bank, Poverty Reduction and Economic Management Network, Policy Research Working Paper 5052, September 2009.

fDi Report 2012: Global Greenfield Investment Trends, April 2012.

'FDI: The Glass is Full One Day, Empty the Next', Charles Clover, *Financial Times,* October 2011.

'Foreign Investment into China Slows', *Forbes,* 19 January 2012.

G-20 Protection in the Wake of the Great Recession, International Chamber of Commerce, 28 June 2010.

'Generation Mobile: Securing Top Talent for FDI', *OCO Global Annual Report 2011/12,* October 2011.

Getting Our Way: 500 Years of Adventure and Intrigue – the Inside Story of British Diplomacy, Christopher Meyer, Weidenfeld & Nicholson, 2009.

Getting Prepared: Economic Development in a Transforming Energy Economy, International Economic Development Council, June 2010.

Global Competitiveness Report 2011–2012, World Economic Forum, September 2011.

Global Outlook Report 2010, fDi Markets.

Great Brand Stories: Brand America, Simon Anholt and Jeremy Hildreth, Palgrave Macmillan, March 2010.

'How Africa is Becoming the New Asia', Jerry Guo, *Newsweek*, 1 March 2010.

How to Brand Nations, Cities and Destinations: A Planning Book for Place Branding, Teemu Moilanen and Sepo Rainisto, Palgrave Macmillan, 2009.

'How to Generate Leads using LinkedIn', *HubSpot*, September 2011.

'Huawei Said to Lose Out on U.S. Assets Despite Higher Offers', Serena Saitto and Jeffrey McCracken, Bloomberg, http://www.bloomberg.com/news/2010-08-02/huawei-said-to-be-stymied-in-purchase-of-u-s-assets-on-security-concerns.html, 3 August 2010 (accessed 9 July 2012).

Investing in a Rebound: The 2010 FDI Confidence Index, A.T. Kearney, 2010.

Investment Trends Monitor no. 8, UNCTAD, 24 January 2012.

Latin America's Decade? FDI Trends and Perspectives, Sergio Barraza, OCO Global, April 2012.

Libya's Year Zero: Finding Opportunity as a Country Rebuilds, Economist Intelligence Unit, November 2011.

Lions On the Move: The Progress and Potential of African Economies, McKinsey Global Institute, 2010.

Nation Branding: Concepts, Issues, Practice, Keith Dinnie, Butterworth-Heinemann, 2008.

'Partnership with CISCO & Imperial in Tech City', http://www.ucl.ac.uk/enterprise/enterprise-news/cp-archive/citiesofthefuture, UCL Enterprise, 7 December 2011 (accessed 9 July 2012).

'Petrobras to Sell $65 Billion Stock in Record Offer', Brian Ellsworth, Reuters, http://www.reuters.com/article/idUSTRE6821FX20100903, 3 September 2010 (accessed 9 July 2012).

Places, Simon Anholt, Palgrave Macmillan, 2009.

'President Obama Issues Call to Action to Invest in America at White House "Insourcing American Jobs" Forum', White House press release, http://www.whitehouse.gov/the-press-office/2012/01/11/president-obama-issues-call-action-invest-america-white-house-insourcing?goback=%2Egmp_4046478%2Egde_4046478_member_89358601, 11 January 2012 (accessed 9 July 2012).

QS World University Rankings 2011/2012, Quacquarelli Symonds, September 2011.

'Rebranding Nigeria', Charles O'Tudor, http://nation-branding. info/2009/03/04/re-branding-nigeria/, 4 March 2009 (accessed 9 July 2012).

Restart: Ernst & Young's 2011 European Attractiveness Survey, Ernst & Young, June 2011.

'Russia Warned Over Intimidation', http://news.bbc.co.uk/1/hi/uk_ politics/7191411.stm, 8 January 2008 (accessed 9 July 2012).

'Selling the State: State Branding as a Political Resource in South Africa', Jeremy Youde, *Place Branding and Public Diplomacy*, vol. 5, no. 2, May 2009.

Serve the People: The New Landscape of Foreign Investment into China, Economist Intelligence Unit, January 2012.

Sovereign Brands Study 2010, Hill & Knowlton and Penn Schoen Berland, May 2010.

'Subsidies for Airbus Illegal, Says WTO', Joshua Chaffin, FT.com, http:// www.ft.com/cms/s/0/624f7e0c-845e-11df-9cbb-00144feabdc0. html#axzz1Dr7OIz00, 30 June 2010 (accessed 9 July 2010).

Technology and Innovation Report, UNCTAD, November 2011.

The fDi Report 2012 – Global Greenfield Investment Trends, Financial Times, April 2012.

'The French Strategic Investment Fund: A Creative Approach to Complement SWF Regulation or Mere Protectionism?', Jean-Rodolphe W. Fiechter, *Journal of Applied Economy*, vol. 3, 'Critical Regulation', April 2010.

The Global Talent Index Report: The Outlook to 2015, Heidrick & Struggles, April 2011.

The Middle of the Pyramid: Dynamics of the Middle Class in Africa, African Development Bank, http://www.afdb.org/fileadmin/uploads/afdb/ Documents/Publications/The%20Middle%20of%20the%20Pyramid_The%20 Middle%20of%20the%20Pyramid.pdf, 20 April 2011 (accessed 9 July 2012).

The Olympics and Economics 2012, Goldman Sachs, July 2012.

The Shadow Market, Eric J. Weiner, Scribner, 2010.

The World is Bumpy: Globalization and New Strategies for Growth, Ernst & Young, January 2012.

Third COMESA Investment Forum: Connecting Africa to the World, Conference Report, IC Publications, May 2010.

Towards New Arrangements for State Ownership in the Middle East and North Africa, OECD, March 2012.

Tracking Global Trends: How Six Key Developments are Shaping the Business World, Ernst & Young, 2011.

'Way-C Tablet, the First African iPad Rival, Goes On Sale in Congo', Erin Conway-Smith, globalpost, http://www.globalpost.com/dispatches/globalpost-blogs/weird-wide-web/african-ipad-way-c-tablet-congo-verone-mankou, 30 January 2012 (accessed 9 July 2012).

When Two Worlds Meet: How High-growth Market Companies are Changing International Business, Economist Intelligence Unit and UK Trade & Investment, September 2011.

World Energy Outlook, International Energy Agency, 2010.

World Investment Report 2010, UNCTAD, July 2010.

World Investment Report 2011, UNCTAD, July 2011.

World Investment Report 2012, UNCTAD, July 2012.

'WTO Rules Boeing Had Illegal Subsidies', Peggy Hollinger, FT.com, http://www.ft.com/cms/s/0/380c7d6c-2d86-11e0-8f53-00144feab49a.html#axzz1Dr7OIz00, 31 January 2011 (accessed 9 July 2012).

Index

2Wire 49
3Com 49, 59

A.T. Kearney FDI Confidence Index
    2007 Index 13, 14, 17, 18, 20
    2010 Index 8, 9, 10, 11–12, 13,
        15, 17, 18, 20, 60, 88
    2012 Index 8, 9, 10, 13, 14, 15,
        17, 18, 20, 24, 75
    overview 64
AAR consortium 70–71
Abu Dhabi 20
accountability 51
Addict-o-matic 83
Africa 4, 16, 23–5, 27, 38–41, 48,
    53–5, 75, 78, 89–90, 91, 95
African Development Bank 54
Aldi 58
Ali, Ben 58
agriculture 46
Airbus 45
America, see United States
American International Group 40
Angola 24
Anholt, Simon 64
Anholt-GfK Roper
    City Brands Index 64–5
    Nation Brands Index 36, 64–5
apartheid 37, 74

Apple 29
Arab Spring 21, 34, 58
architecture 21, 29
Argentina 46
Armani 29
Asia-Pacific region 9–10, 12, 39, 61, 90
Association of Executive Search
        Consultants (AESC) 90
Austria 15
authenticity 28, 32
automotive industry 47
aviation industry 45–6

Baidu 39
bailouts 14, 20, 57
Banca Popolare di Milano 71
Bangalore 88
Beijing 10, 61, 75, 88
Belgium 11, 95
benchmarking 63, 66, 87
Berkshire Hathaway 46
Berlusconi, Silvio 71
'Best Countries in the World'
        (Newsweek) 65
BG Group 17
Blogdigger 83
blogs 80, 81
BMW 29
BNP Paribas 71

Boeing 45
Bouazizi, Mohammed 58
BP 14, 70–71, 80
brain drain 59
brain gain 33, 89–92
brand continuity 32
brand ownership 80
brands, *see* corporate brands;
        place brands
Brazil 17–18, 45, 75, 85, 90, 91
BRICS (Brazil, Russia, India, China,
        South Africa) 1, 4, 12–13, 24,
        68, 74–5
British Council 13–14
broad elites 33, 50
Brown, Gordon 11
Buffett, Warren 46
Bulgari 71

California 29
Cambridge University 59
Cameron, David 11, 62, 69
Canada 88
capacity-building 8, 66, 70
catalyst effect 3
CEMEX 19
Chile 18
China 4, 9–10, 34, 39, 45, 46, 48–9, 50,
        53–4, 57, 59, 61, 69, 74, 75, 85
China Mobile 39
Chongqing 10
Churchill, Winston 23
Cisco 92
Cities and Regions of the Future
        (fDi Intelligence) 65
City Brands Index (Anholt-GfK Roper)
        64–5
CIVETS (Colombia, Indonesia,
        Vietnam, Egypt, Turkey and
        South Africa) 75
clean technology 4
clusters 3, 56, 59, 61–2
Coca-Cola 17

collaboration 29
Colombia 18
colonialism 23, 54
Commonwealth Games 10, 75–6
communications strategies 40–41, 51;
        see also marketing
Community of Latin American
        Countries (CELAC) 17
competitor analysis 28
Congo 78, 95
Copenhagen 30–31
Copenhagen Capacity 30, 62
Copenhagen Criteria 15
corporate advocacy 62–3
corporate brands 29, 39, 80
corruption 13–14, 32, 37, 54–5
costs 60, 65
country of origin effect 22, 39, 42, 50
creation 83–4
culture 64, 65
Czech Pegas 35
Czech Republic 45

Davos 29, 92
Deepwater Horizon disaster 80
Delhi 10, 75–6
Denmark 31, 62
destination heat maps 1, 2
destination marketing, *see* marketing
diaspora 29, 33
        returning 33, 89–92
Digital Shoreditch 62
diplomacy 47, 52; *see also* public
        diplomacy
domestic investment 3, 19, 44–5
Dubai 6, 19–23, 31, 40, 61, 88
Dubai Ports World 40, 42, 44, 70, 73
Duggan, Mark 58

Ease of Doing Business Index
        (World Bank) 18, 31, 63
East African Community (EAC) 16, 38
East Anglia 59

economic development organisations
3, 30–31, 35–6, 37, 59, 62, 65, 92
economic downturn 7–25, 31, 46, 48,
57–8
Economic Freedom Index (Heritage
Foundation) 18, 66
Economist 74
Economist Intelligence Unit (EIU) 10
Liveability Ranking Report 65–6
EDF 71
Edison 71
education 4, 9, 33, 65, 95
Egypt 26, 34–5, 58
Emirates 61
Enterprise Florida 85–6
entrepreneurship 10, 33, 39, 92–3, 95
Ernst & Young 4
Europe 11–12, 14–16, 44–5, 57, 85,
90–91
European Commission 16, 72
European Court of Justice (ECJ) 16
European Organisation for Nuclear
Research (CERN) 35
European Parliament 16
European Union (EU) 14, 15–16, 45,
52, 57, 71–2, 90–91
eurozone 14–15, 16, 57, 79
evaluation 84
executive relocation 14, 59, 66, 93
exports 64
ExxonMobil 14, 70

Facebook 80, 81, 85, 92
familiarity 22, 50, 52
fast-moving consumer goods (FMCG)
17, 47
favourability 22, 50, 52
FDI Confidence Index, *see* A.T. Kearney
FDI Confidence Index
fDi Intelligence
Cities and Regions of the Future
65
FIFA World Cup 17, 37, 74, 75, 90

financial services industry 11
Financial Times 65
France 12, 15, 44–5, 46, 57, 58, 71–2,
85–6, 95
free trade agreements (FTAs) 18

G20 countries 43
Gartner 34
Geneva 35
geopolitics 48
Germany 12, 15, 45, 46, 57
Ghana 89
Global Competitiveness index (WEF)
18, 36, 64, 91
Global Peace Index (IEP) 66
Global Trade Alert 46
globalisation 22
Google 92
Google Alerts 83
governance 15, 51, 64
governments, role of 69–73
Greece 12, 14, 15–16, 57
growth 19, 23–4, 39, 95
Grupo Financiero Imbrusa 19
Guangzhou 10

healthcare 65
heat maps 1, 2
hedge funds 50
heritage 64
Heritage Foundation
Economic Freedom Index 18, 66
higher education 4, 9, 33, 59, 61, 89
Hill & Knowlton / Hill+Knowlton
Strategies ix, xi, 33, 50
historical contexts 23, 47–8
Homecoming Revolution 89
Hong Kong 48, 61, 88, 90
Huawei 49
HubSpot
State of Inbound Marketing Report
80–81
human resources 59, 65–6, 87–92

human rights 54–5, 66, 75
Hungary 12, 39, 85

IKEA 13
Imperial College, London 92
India 9, 10, 34, 39, 46–7, 59, 61, 75–6,
  85, 95
Indonesia 61
Information Technology Industry
  Development Agency (ITIDA) 34
infrastructure 9, 21, 53, 61, 65
innovation 3, 17–18, 33, 35, 44, 92–3,
  95
Institute for Economics and Peace 66
insurance industry 46
interaction 83–4
International Economic Development
  Council (IEDC) 82
International Energy Agency (IEA) 4, 31
international events 10, 17–18, 29,
  37, 74, 75–6, 90
International Marketing Council
  (South Africa) 37, 73–4
International Monetary Fund (IMF) 57
International Office for Migration
  (IOM) 89
international relations 47–8, 52, 70,
  73–4
Invest in Skåne 62
investment banks 50, 52
investment promotion, *see* marketing;
  place brands
investor confidence 7, 8, 10–12,
  13–14, 15, 18, 19, 20–21, 22,
  34, 57–8, 62, 64, 91–2
investor retention 62–3
Ireland 12, 15, 57
IT industry 34, 62
Italy 12, 15–16, 29, 45, 57, 71–2
iWiW 85

Jaguar 39
Japan 29

job creation 3, 44, 47, 93–4
joint ventures 14, 70–71

Kenya 16, 24
Kinnock, Stephen 13
kiranas 46
Kirk, Ron 48–9
knowledge transfer 66, 70

La Caixa 19
Lactalis 71–2, 73
Land Rover 39
Latin America 16–19, 90
Latvia 12
Libya 58
LinkedIn 80, 81, 85, 86
Liveability Ranking Report (EIU)
  65–6
Litvinenko, Alexander 13
location 61
London 56, 58, 88, 90
LVMH 71

Malaysia 61
Mandela, Nelson 37
Manpower 91
market potential 60–61
marketing 27–9, 73–4, 82–7;
  see also brands
Marks & Spencer 47
Medicon Valley 62, 92
MENA (Middle East and North Africa)
  1, 20, 21
Mercosur 16–17
mergers and acquisitions (M&A) 13,
  15, 44
Mexico 18–19, 75
MICE approach 82–4
micro-entrepreneurship 92
Microsoft 59
Middle East 20–21, 40, 58, 61, 66, 79
mobile technology 80, 81, 87–8
monitoring 83

Monitter 83
Montréal 88
Montréal International 88
Motorola 49
Mubudala 45
Munich 29

Nation Brands Index (Anholt-GfK
    Roper) 36, 64–5
national identities 47–8
national security 40, 44, 49
natural resources 13, 17, 53, 75
neo-imperialism 23, 53–5
Netherlands 11, 15
New York 88, 90
Newsweek 89–90
    'Best Countries in the World' 65
Next 11 (N11) countries 18, 75
Nigeria 24, 31–2, 89, 90, 91
North American Free Trade
    Association (NAFTA) 18

Obama, Barack 19, 20, 79
objectives 28, 32
OCO Global 88–9
Olympic Games 17, 29, 75, 90
Oman 51
O'Neill, Jim 74–5
onshoring 19
opium wars 48
Orkut 85
O'Tudor, Charles 32
outsourcing 34

P&O 40
Paris 58, 88
Parmalat 71–2, 73
peace 57–8, 66
Pearl River delta 61
PepsiCo 14
Persian Gulf 40, 61
Peterson Institute for International
    Economics (PIIE) 43

Petrobras 17
Philippines 39, 61
Pittsburgh 31
place brands 3, 5, 21–3, 27–41, 64–5,
    73–6, 86
Poland 15, 90–91
populism 47, 48
Portugal 15–16, 57
Presence Switzerland 35–6
productivity 3, 17–18
proposition-based marketing 86–7
protectionism 5, 40, 43–53, 69, 71–2
public diplomacy 73–6;
    see also diplomacy
public relations (PR) 80
Putin, Vladimir 48, 70

Qualcomm 59
quality of life 31, 65–6, 93

rankings 63–7
Reconnect Africa 89
renewable energy 4
repatriation 33, 89–92
reputation 3, 5, 21–3, 25, 27–41,
    73–6, 80
research and development (R&D) 3, 33
Rosneft 14, 70
Russia 1, 12–14, 46, 47–8, 70–71, 75, 85

Samsung 39
São Paolo 90, 91
Sarkozy, Nicolas 44
Schwab, Klaus 92
SelectUSA 20, 44
Shadow Market, The (Weiner) 49–50
Shanghai 61, 88
Silicon Fen 59
Silicon Roundabout 62
Singapore 31, 59, 88, 90
social media 4, 33, 35, 62–3, 79–86,
    87, 93
Sony 29, 39, 59

South Africa 24, 37, 32, 68, 73–6, 89
South Korea 39, 75
sovereign brands 33, 50
sovereign debt crisis 14, 57, 79
sovereign wealth funds (SWFs) 33, 44–5, 49–51, 52, 70, 73
Spain 11, 12, 15–16, 45, 57
sporting events 10, 17–18, 29, 37, 74, 75–6, 90
stability 7, 15, 19, 33, 58, 65
state aid 45–6
state-driven investments 70
State of Inbound Marketing Report (HubSpot) 80–81
state-owned assets 70
State General Reserve Fund (Oman) 51
Strategic Investment Fund (SIF) 44–5
strategic partnerships 12
subprime mortgage crisis 7, 19
supply chain development 3
Sweden 62
Switzerland 11, 15, 35–7
SWOT analysis 28
Sydney 88
Syria 58

Tanzania 16
TATA 39
taxation 60
Tech City UK 56, 62, 92
Tech City Investment Organisation (TCIO) 62
technology transfer 3, 44
Tesco 47
Tetley Tea 39
Tianji 85
Time magazine 74
Toshiba 59
tourism 17, 22, 27, 32, 64, 73
Toyota 39
trade disputes 45, 47
transparency 51, 76, 79

transport links 61
Treaty of Nanking 48
Tremonti, Guilio 71
TripAdvisor effect 62–3
Tunisia 58
Turkey 75
Tutu, Desmond 37
Twilert 83
Twitter 35, 80, 81, 83, 85, 86

Uganda 16
UK Trade and Investment (UKTI) 29, 62, 86
Unisfair 80
United Arab Emirates (UAE) 20, 40, 45; *see also* Dubai
United Kingdom 10–12, 15, 45, 46, 48, 58, 59, 69, 86
United Nations Conference on Trade and Development (UNCTAD) 13, 36, 57, 91
United States 10, 11, 18–20, 22–3, 40, 44, 45, 48–9, 57, 59, 66, 79, 90
universities 4, 59, 61, 89, 92
University College London (UCL) 92

Viadeo 85–6
Vietnam 39, 61
violence 58
virtual events 80, 81
vkontakte 85

wage premium 3, 54
Wall Street Journal 66
Wal-Mart 17, 47
Way-C tablet 78, 95
websites 51
Weiner, Eric J. 49–50
WikiLeaks 76
Wimm-Bill-Dann 14
World Bank 30
    Ease of Doing Business index 18, 31, 63

World Economic Forum (WEF) 29, 92
    Global Competitiveness index 18, 36, 64, 91
World Trade Organisation (WTO) 14, 45

Xing 85

Youde, Jeremy 74
YouTube 93

Zuckerberg, Mark 92
Zuma, Jacob 74, 75

For Product Safety Concerns and Information please contact our EU
representative GPSR@taylorandfrancis.com Taylor & Francis Verlag GmbH,
Kaufingerstraße 24, 80331 München, Germany

Printed and bound by CPI Group (UK) Ltd, Croydon, CR0 4YY

01/05/2025

01858375-0001